BIZARRE

TRUE CRIME

VOLUME 9

Ben Oakley

"When the going gets weird, the weird turn pro." - Hunter S. Thompson

Bizarre True Crime Volume 9

20 wild and shocking
true crime stories.

The Bizarre True Crime books can be read in any order. You don't need to have read the previous books to enjoy this one.

This is the second book of Season Two, and the ninth book in the series overall. There are seven books per season, released over the course of twelve months.

Season One: Volumes 1-7

Season Two: Volumes 8-14

1. The Black Dahlia Murder

It is perhaps the most famous unsolved cold case in history, so get your sleuthing hat on as we take a deep dive into the horrific murder of Elizabeth Short.

2. The Vampire of Nuremberg

A deaf and mute occultist, believing necrophilia could make him handsome, killed three people and drank their blood, before he was caught kissing a corpse in a graveyard.

3. The Bloodthirsty Harpe Brothers

Two men in search of a better future on the American frontier, became bloodthirsty criminals who claimed at least 39 lives, and in folklore are known as America's first serial killers.

4. Unthankful Brother Murdered with an Axe

A drunk man killed his brother with an axe as he slept because he forgot to say thank you for cooking dinner, in a cautionary tale where good manners mean the difference between life and death.

5. The Serpent

An unusual serial killer and lifetime criminal, who claimed the lives of dozens of western tourists travelling the hippie trail, killing to cover his tracks and live off the proceeds of his victims.

6. Tattingstone Suitcase Murder

A young man disappeared in London only to turn up dead ten days later, chopped up into eight pieces and left in two suitcases on a Suffolk farm, leading to a half-century long investigation.

7. The Death of Kirsty MacColl

Famed for duetting the Christmas song, Fairytale of New York, Kirsty died in a suspicious boating accident, leading her family to believe there was a cover up to protect the real culprit.

8. The Blackburn Cult

Also known as the Great Eleven, the Blackburn Cult included strange rituals, animal sacrifice, the attempted resurrection of a teenage princess, and a con by two failed actresses.

9. The Tall Tale of Toby Cole

A deaf mute teenage girl stumbled into a school having escaped a satanic cult, but there was something about her story that didn't add up, leading to an extraordinary revelation.

10. The Severed Feet of the Salish Sea

The unsettling discovery of severed feet and legs washing up along the Salish Sea led to rumours of serial killers and aliens, but the truth was even more disturbing.

11. Maniac Cop: The Murder of Missy Bevers

In one of modern times most eerie unsolved cold cases, a fitness instructor was killed in a local church by a person dressed in police SWAT gear.

12. Murderous King of the Osage Hills

After the suspicious deaths of many Osage Indians, the FBI went undercover and unearthed a conspiracy involving multiple murder, insurance fraud, and a belief the Wild West was still alive.

13. The Jammie Dodger Robbery

In a robbery worthy of bizarre true crime, a gang stole £20,000 worth of Jammie Dodgers, and when they were sentenced, shouted out 'anyone want a biscuit?'

14. The Wartime Ripper

During wartime London, as the German bombs were raining down, a serial killer was at work who brought a new kind of darkness to the cold and lonely streets of the British Capital.

15. The Pendle Witches

In the summer of 1612, ten witches, six from two rival families, were found guilty of murder and witchcraft and executed at Gallows Hill, in one of the best-recorded witch trials in history.

16. Burning of Mary Channing

A young woman obsessed with free money, parties, and multiple lovers, poisoned her husband and was burned at the stake for her troubles in front of thousands of people.

17. Codename Piccadilly and the Umbrella Murder

While waiting for a bus in London, a Bulgarian writer and journalist was assassinated after being stabbed in the thigh with the poisonous tip of an umbrella, by an assassin codenamed Piccadilly.

18. The Monster Butler & The Sidekick

Scottish serial killer Archibald Hall, known as The Monster Butler, killed five people in the late 1970s while working for the British upper class, with help from his sidekick, Kitto.

19. The Ice Cream Wars

In 1980s Glasgow, rival criminal gangs were using ice cream vans to sell drugs and stolen goods, leading to the mass murder of six people and a man gluing himself to the railings of Buckingham Palace.

20. That's Not Cocaine!

Believing they had stumbled upon a goldmine, three thieves stole two large jars of cocaine, but after snorting it, they realised they were urns that contained the ashes of one human and two dogs.

The Black Dahlia Murder

It is perhaps the most famous unsolved cold case in history, so get your sleuthing hat on as we take a deep dive into the horrific murder of Elizabeth Short.

Along with the murder of six-year-old beauty queen JonBenét Ramsay (Bizarre Volume 5), the Black Dahlia is head and shoulders above the rest when it comes to the most famous cold cases and unsolved murders of all time.

Unlike the Ramsay murder which has a limited amount of suspects, the Black Dahlia involves an entire spectrum of potential killers, reaching into the heart of Hollywood itself, along with a potential cover-up to hide the true face behind the killing.

Not only is the Black Dahlia murder unsolved, but it is also a horrific case where the victim, 22-year-old aspiring actress Elizabeth Short, was mutilated by her killer and drained of blood before being cut in half at the waist, leading to some wild theories that we'll look at shortly.

Elizabeth was born in 1924 Boston, Massachusetts, the third of five daughters to hard-working parents. Her father, Cleo, was a miniature golf course builder who had established quite the business until the stock market crash of 1929 wiped out his entire savings.

When Elizabeth was six, Cleo drove to Charlestown Bridge in Boston and allegedly took his own life by jumping into the river below, his car was found on the side of the bridge. Elizabeth's mother, who had stayed at home to look after the children, was forced to become an accountant to make ends meet.

Due to the alleged death of her father, Elizabeth got into a lot of trouble at school and then began to suffer from severe asthma and bronchitis. At the age of 15, she underwent major lung surgery and was told by the doctors to move to a milder climate in the south to prevent further issues, leading to her spending the winters in Miami.

In 1942, when Elizabeth was 18, a bombshell letter landed on her mother's doorstep. The letter was from Cleo, apologising for faking his own death, and stating he was alive and well in California. Due to her condition, Elizabeth decided to move to California to live with the father she assumed was dead. And it doesn't get any less weird from here on out.

Moving around

Her father was working at a U.S. Navy shipyard in San Francisco and living nearby. Due to the way he had faked his death and the mental distress it had caused Elizabeth, they argued to the point that she moved out to Santa Barbara and got a job working at a military retail store.

This put her in contact with numerous members of the military, and due to her supposed good looks, she was propositioned many times but fell for an Air Force sergeant who ended up abusing her, causing her to elope again.

She was arrested in Santa Barbara in September 1943 for underage drinking at a local bar and was ordered to go back home to Boston, but instead went to Florida where she knew the area well due to spending her winter's there.

In Florida, she met and fell in love with Major Matthew Gordon, who proposed to her by letter after his plane crashed in India during the Second World War. But Gordon never made it home, as another plane he was on crashed and killed everyone on board.

Unable to settle down, and with her relationships ending in the most horrific of ways, Elizabeth decided to move back to California and relocated to Los Angeles in July 1946, where she stayed briefly with another military man, Joseph Fickling.

Six months before her death, she got a job working as a waitress near Hollywood and rented a room directly behind a nightclub called Florentine Gardens, on Hollywood Boulevard. But her newfound dreams of becoming a Hollywood actress were cut down in January 1947.

Drained of blood

On the morning of 15th January 1947, Betty Bersinger was walking through the as yet undeveloped Leimert Park with her three-year-old daughter, Anne, on the way to a shoe repair shop, when she noticed something unusual on the grass up ahead.

Because the park was undeveloped, there were normally items of trash that people had disposed of but Betty thought it odd that someone had thrown out a broken mannequin. As she got closer, she discovered it was no mannequin but the mutilated corpse of a female.

She grabbed Anne from the buggy and ran to a nearby house to raise the alarm, kicking off a case that has held the public's attention ever since. In just a few minutes, the authorities were on the scene, unsure exactly what they were looking at.

Perhaps there's no such thing as an ordinary murder, but Elizabeth's murder was far from ordinary. She had been cut in half at the waist and some of her organs had been removed along with her intestines. A tattoo of a rose had been sliced off and placed inside her vagina.

Her face had been cut from the corners of her mouth to her ears, creating a smile-like effect. Much of her body had been slashed with a knife and sections of flesh had been cut away from her breasts and thighs. The lower half of her body was positioned one foot away from her upper half, with her intestines tucked underneath her buttocks.

Her mannequin-like white look was caused by the fact there was no blood found in her body – she had been completely drained. There was also no blood at the scene and both sections of her body had been washed clean by the killer before being dumped on the grass, approximately 12 hours before.

Police were able to lift Elizabeth's fingerprints which were sent to the FBI through an early version of the fax machine. Within an hour, the identification of Elizabeth came back, made easy due to her time working in a military shop and her arrest for underage drinking. Police had the name but had no idea where to begin.

The Black Dahlia

The medical examiners determined that Elizabeth had been killed on the night of 14th January to the early hours of the 15th. During the autopsy, ligature marks were found on her ankles, wrists, and neck, meaning she had been tied up before being killed.

Her body had been cut in half at the waist with medical precision after her death, separating her between the second and third lower vertebrae. It was concluded she had been killed with a heavy blow to the head and was most likely raped beforehand, though it has never been proven.

Then the press got involved and began muddying the waters, leading to sensationalism that has never been far from the public eye. In a terrible act of 'journalism', reporters from the Los Angeles Examiner, who had found out Elizabeth's name, contacted her mother in Boston by phone.

They told her that Elizabeth had won a beauty contest and were looking for more information to run a story, but there was no beauty contest, they were tricking Elizabeth's mother into handing over private information they could publish.

After they had got all the information they needed, they told her that Elizabeth was in fact, dead. The reporters then offered plane fares to Los Angeles and accommodation in order to keep Elizabeth's mother talking only to them.

Both the Examiner and the Los Angeles Herald-Express ran sensationalised stories about Elizabeth, in that she always wore tight black clothing, was an adventuress, a Hollywood prowler, and was promiscuous with men, all leading to the moniker of the Black Dahlia.

The moniker was created from a film released in 1946 called The Blue Dahlia. Blue was changed to black after the press ran the stories about the tight black clothing Elizabeth would wear. From then on, Elizabeth would forever be known as the Black Dahlia.

Cleveland Torso Murderer

Between 1935 and 1938, in Cleveland, Ohio, a serial killer known as the Cleveland Torso Murderer, killed at least 13 people, both women and men. The victims were usually drifters or people from lower class backgrounds, who were easy to find in Depression-era Cleveland.

Every single one of the victims were beheaded and dismembered, with some of them being cut in half at the waist. Some of the corpses had been cleaned and treated with a chemical, similar to how Elizabeth had been cut in half and cleaned before being disposed of.

Many of the heads of the victims were never located, and most bodies were only found months after their death which made identification impossible. The killer, who has remained unidentified to this day, boldly placed the remains of two of his victims in front of the city hall, where the offices of the public safety director, who were investigating him, were located.

The killings stopped around 1938, but in Pennsylvania between 1940 and 1942, more beheaded and dismembered victims were found in boxcars and in swamps, leading some researchers to suggest that the Cleveland Torso Murderer had simply moved on to another state.

It was deemed possible that the killer moved from the East coast to the West and killed Elizabeth in Los Angeles. However, the victim selection was very different. Although Elizabeth was working as a waitress, she was not a drifter or of a lower class, and at the time it was easier to get away with murder in less built up areas. Like the killer of Elizabeth, the Cleveland Torso Murderer remains unidentified.

The Lipstick Murderer

One month after Elizabeth's murder, on 10th February, the body of Jeanne French was discovered in Los Angeles. At 8am that morning, a construction worker noticed a pile of women's clothes just away from the sidewalk, but upon closer inspection, he came across Jeanne's beaten and brutalised body.

Jeanne had been beaten and stomped to death, and was found covered in bruises, which had led to severe blood loss. As she lay dying, the killer removed her red lipstick from her handbag and wrote a message on her torso that read, *'Fuck you, P.D.'*

The press interpreted it as B.D. (Black Dahlia) and connected Jeanne's murder to Elizabeth's. The police were unconvinced that the murders were caused by the same person and were seeking two different culprits for the crimes. To this day, despite multiple suspects, Jeanne's murder also remains unsolved.

Over the years, many people came forward to confess to the crime but they have all been false confessions, those seeking their 15 minutes of fame, linking them to the most famous unsolved murder of all time. But even with the confessions, the police struggled from the very beginning.

Police interviewed hundreds of suspects who had tenuous links to Elizabeth, from other waitresses, nightclub goers, ex-military cohorts and former partners but they were not able to gain enough evidence to charge any one of them.

Mark Hansen and the letters

The investigation directly after the murder yielded minimal returns. Police found a heel print near the body that didn't belong to Elizabeth, and a cement sack that contained remnants of bloody water, which was suspected to be how the body was moved.

Six days after the murder, the Los Angeles Examiner received a phone call from a man claiming to be the killer. He congratulated reporters on the paper's coverage of the case and claimed he would be sending some of Elizabeth's belongings to the paper's offices in the mail to prove his claim.

The phoned-in confession was discarded until three days later on the 24th when a package turned up at the Examiner's offices. A letter made from words cut out of newspapers read, '*Los Angeles Examiner and other Los Angeles papers, here is Dahlia's belongings, letter to follow.*'

Inside the package were Elizabeth's birth certificate, her business cards, photographs, names written on various pieces of paper and an address book. The book had the name Mark Hansen embossed on the cover. All the items and the packaging had been wiped clean with gasoline.

Partial fingerprints were lifted but were destroyed in transit and have never been recovered. That same day, a handbag and shoes were discovered in a bin near to where Elizabeth's body had been found but they had also been cleaned with gasoline and there were no fingerprints. It has long remained uncertain whether they belonged to Elizabeth or not.

A handwritten letter arrived at the Examiner's offices on January 26th that read, '*here it is. Turning in Wed. January 29, 10 a.m. Had my fun at police. Black Dahlia Avenger.*' It also included a location that the police went to at 10am on the 29th but the writer of the letter never showed. On 14th March, a suicide note was found in a shoe with clothing on a nearby shoreline.

It read, '*to whom it may concern: I have waited for the police to capture me for the Black Dahlia killing but have not. I am too much of a coward to turn myself in, so this is the best way out for me. I couldn't help myself for that, or this. Sorry, Mary.*'

Though the author of the note was never named, there was a Mark Hansen living in Los Angeles and was known to Elizabeth, as she had stayed at his home with friends on occasion. Hansen was a nightclub owner and owned the Florentine Gardens nightclub, the same nightclub that Elizabeth was renting a room behind.

A friend of Elizabeth's claimed she had rejected Hansen's sexual advances which may have given reason for Hansen to kill her. But despite being a suspect, Hansen was removed from the suspect list due to lack of evidence.

The Black Dahlia Avenger

After interviewing a pool of 750 suspects, the investigation quickly came to an end as there was minimal evidence to go on, and fewer suspects. Elizabeth's death became a cold case within a few months and would eventually fall into true crime legend.

One suspect that has stood the test of time, among some researchers, is the physician George Hodel, who ran a venereal disease clinic in Los Angeles during the 1940s. Hodel was on a list of six prime suspects the police had drawn up at the time.

They had even gone as far as bugging his home but their investigation yielded no results. Hodel died in 1999, having forever remained on the suspect list. But in 2003, Hodel's son, Steve, who was a former police officer, wrote a book called 'The Black Dahlia Avenger: A Genius for Murder: The True Story.'

In it, he claims his own father was the killer. Steve suggests that the handwriting in the letters sent to the Examiner's offices were a match to his late father. He also found numerous photos of women who looked like Elizabeth in his father's personal photo albums.

The fact that Hodel was a physician, meant he would have had the medical experience needed to cut the body in half with medical precision, drain it of blood, and wash it clean. Hodel trained at a University that taught hemicorporectomy, the technique used for cutting the body through the spine.

Steve also found a receipt dated a few days before the murder for a large bag of concrete. It was claimed to have been the same size and brand as the empty bag found near the body. Despite the mounting evidence, sceptics refused to believe it because Steve had also linked his father to the Zodiac Killer.

However, while fact-checking the book, a Los Angeles Times columnist requested official police files from the case, including the transcribed audio recordings from Hodel's home. Within the transcribes, the reporter found shocking evidence.

At 8.25pm, a few days after the killing, one of the transcribes reads, 'Woman screamed. Woman screamed again.' Then later that day, Hodel was talking to an unknown person when he said the following.

'Realize there was nothing I could do, put a pillow over her head and cover her with a blanket. Get a taxi. Expired 12:59. They thought there was something fishy. Anyway, now they may have figured it out. Killed her.' Then, *'supposing I did kill the Black Dahlia. They couldn't prove it now. They can't talk to my secretary anymore because she's dead.'*

This assumed that if Hodel had killed Elizabeth, that his secretary, Ruth Spaulding, had found out about it, and he killed her to remove a potential witness. Incidentally, Hodel was a suspect in Ruth's death but was never charged as there was no evidence to prove it.

Labyrinthine case

Despite the evidence they had, the police at the time either didn't check the transcripts properly or were covering up Hodel being the suspect, as has been insinuated by modern researchers. But if the Hodel evidence is purely circumstantial and unproven, then who did kill Elizabeth and why did they do it?

There have been many false confessions, and many names put forward by various researchers and authors but none have come to anything substantial. In 2017, a British author named Piu Eatwell, proposed a different theory, that the killer was hotel worker and former mortician assistant, Leslie Duane Dillon.

Dillon was associated with Mark Hansen and Finis Brown, a lead detective on the original case, who was allegedly corrupt. Dillon was originally on the suspect list but was quickly removed, with the author of the book suggesting it was because of his association with Hansen and Brown.

An interview with a former police officer, claimed that his father, who was also an officer with the LAPD gangster squad, overhead a damning conversation. His father was talking to other members of the squad and said that they knew the killer was Dillon but he had orchestrated the murder with Hansen and another man named Jeff Connors.

The reason for the murder was that Elizabeth may have found out about a hotel robbery scam that Dillon and Hansen were about to be involved in. She was murdered in a room at the Aster Motel in Hollywood, where the owners of the hotel found one of their cabins covered in blood the next day.

It was reported to police, who seemed to ignore it at the time – or cover it up due to their connections with Hansen. One final theory rests on American visual artist, Man Ray, who was known for creating surreal photographic imagery and films, sometimes pornographic in nature.

Some of his work is Cronenberg-like in nature, with contortions of the flesh and female bodies in weirdly horrific poses. To top it all off, he was friends with George Hodel. Maybe, just maybe, his masterpiece was the gory presentation of Elizabeth's body.

But as convincing as many of the theories and suspects are, the Black Dahlia murder remains unsolved and is considered one of the most infamous cold cases in the world. There have been numerous books, films, and TV shows about the murder, all with a different angle.

Murder is one thing but the killer went to great lengths to dismember and mutilate the body to such a degree, knowing it would easily be found. And it is those gory details that will forever remain embedded in the minds of those who enter the labyrinthine case of the Black Dahlia.

FACTS!

The early version of the fax machine used by the FBI was called a Soundphoto, a successor to the Wirephoto, which sent photocell images over ordinary phone lines.

The FBI reported they received over 500 confessions to the murder of Elizabeth, some of which came from soldiers, priests, housewives and bar owners.

In 2019, there were 174,331 violent crimes reported in California. 1,690 of these were for murder.

The Vampire of Nuremberg

A deaf and mute occultist, believing necrophilia could make him handsome, killed three people and drank their blood, before he was caught kissing a corpse in a graveyard.

In the middle of the night on 10th May 1972, in Nuremberg, Germany, morgue attendant George Warmuth spotted a shadowy figure in the graveyard. As he drew closer to see who it was, he recoiled in shock, as the figure was holding a corpse in his arms, locked in a passionate kiss.

George wouldn't know it at the time, but he had stumbled across a triple murderer, necrophile, grave-robber, cannibal, and blood drinker named Kuno Hoffman, known later across Germany and the world as the Vampire of Nuremberg.

Kuno was born in 1931 and raised in a violent household, where his father would abuse him constantly. On one occasion, Kuno was beaten so badly by his father, that it caused him to lose his speech and hearing, making him deaf and mute.

Needless to say, his teenage years were marred with crime and mental health issues, which led to him spending many years in and out of psychiatric hospitals and prisons. He allegedly escaped from 12 psychiatric hospitals throughout the years.

When he was convicted of a theft charge in the early 1960s, Kuno spent nine years in prison. While there, he became obsessed with the occult and satanism, and consumed many books on the subjects, which led to a fascination with rituals involving vampirism and necrophilia.

Copulating with the dead

When he was released from prison, he continued to study books on the occult and satanism, in an effort to understand what he called the occult sciences. For many years, due to his mental health status and disabilities, Kuno had come to believe he was ugly and weak.

The entire purpose of studying the occult was to look for ways to make himself handsome and strong. Unable to hold down a job due to his condition and inability to stick it out, the occult alleviated his loneliness and offered a promise of a new life.

Kuno developed the notion that by performing satanic rituals over corpses and then drinking their blood, he would achieve his goals of becoming handsome and strong. In early 1971, Kuno turned his dreams of perfection into reality. But to attain his dreams, he needed the perfect corpse, and there was no better corpse than someone who had recently died. He perused the local newspapers for obituaries and picked the recently dead who attracted him the most.

Under cover of night, Kuno broke into various graveyards and mortuaries to copulate with the dead. He was able to make copies of cemetery keys and used them to hide among the tombstones before digging up a corpse then stabbing and slicing the body with a razor to retrieve blood.

He would bite the corpses, drink as much of the drying blood as possible and chew the flesh. His real prize, however, were the bodies in the mortuaries, as he believed the blood to be fresher and was able to do things he couldn't always do in the graveyards – engage in necrophilia.

35 corpses

Necrophilia is one of those unsavoury human traits that we rarely hear about, and for some of us, the less we know about it, the better. For the Vampire of Nuremberg, although starting out as a means to an end, he began to enjoy the act and focused his attention on young women who had died in the region – young women he found himself sexually attracted to.

After working out which mortuary their bodies would be held at, he broke in and danced with the dead for as long as he pleased. When morticians and morgue workers turned up for work, they found their recently dead corpses had been sexually assaulted and butchered.

It was estimated that between 1971 and 1972, at least 35 corpses had been attacked in such a way, with some of them dug up in cemeteries. Almost all of the female corpses showed evidence of penetration, with some of them having been beheaded.

By early 1972, police were made aware of the unusual attacks on corpses but had no suspect in sight. Nuremberg wasn't the best of places in the early 1970s due to the fallout of the Second World War but a vampiric necrophile on the loose was certainly abnormal and warranted much attention.

But Kuno was just getting started. As much as he enjoyed consuming the blood of recently dead corpses, he found the quality of blood he drank from the bodies was not quite as good as he wanted and so his attention turned to the living.

Triple murder

On 6th May 1972, 24-year-old Markus Adler and his fiancée, 18-year-old Ruth Lissy, were sitting in their car, on a romantic night out, unaware of the danger nearby. Kuno was watching them from the shadows, gun in hand, ready to claim the freshest of corpses for their blood.

He approached from the darkness and caught the couple off-guard before shooting them dead through the window of the car. He then cut their throats and drank the blood from their lifeless bodies before having sex with Ruth's corpse.

Two days later, empowered with the rush of fresh blood, Kuno went on the prowl for another victim and found a young woman walking alone at night. He approached her from behind and shot her in the back of the head before slicing her arteries and drinking from her body.

She too was raped after death but her name has never been released in Germany, because of various privacy laws. This likely meant she was under the age of 18 at the time of her murder and caused a massive police investigation when her death was linked to the previous two.

Then, on 10th May 1972, with three linked murders in the region, and a serial killer on the loose, cemetery and mortuary workers were put on alert, which led to morgue attendant George Warmuth running a security check on the nearby cemetery.

It was there, he witnessed a man in the shadows holding a corpse in his arms and locked in a passionate embrace. A man the local media had come to call the Vampire of Nuremberg. When Kuno realised he was being watched, he dropped the body, pulled his gun and fired at Warmuth.

Cold-blooded vampirism

The bullet missed Warmuth by inches and he survived the attack but Kuno had eloped. As Kuno ran under the direct moonlight, Warmuth noted everything he could about his appearance, which would lead to Kuno's arrest in the early hours of the following morning.

Police quickly discovered that Kuno had been seen by other witnesses hanging around cemeteries and mortuaries. The witness statements, combined with Kuno's long history of stays in psychiatric hospitals, made him the prime suspect.

Upon his arrest, Kuno readily admitted to the grave robberies, blood drinking, necrophilia, and the three murders. He casually explained that when he found the corpses to be of a low-quality blood-drinking experience, he escalated to murder.

He also claimed he was going to continue killing and drinking blood until the ritual of handsomeness and strength had been achieved. But he admitted at the same time he had come to enjoy the act of blood-drinking as a fetish despite the original intent of rituals.

At his trial, it was suspected that Kuno would be able to plead not guilty on grounds of insanity but it was concluded by the court that Kuno knew the difference between right and wrong and would stand trial for triple murder, grave-robbing, satanism, and copulation with a corpse.

He was sentenced to life in prison in late 1972, where he remained until his death a few years later. Though his cause of death has never been released, it was suspected to be down to complications following consumption of raw human flesh and blood.

While in prison, he asked fellow prisoners and guards if they had access to the blood of virgins to help him live longer. His requests were obviously denied. The Vampire of Nuremberg remains one of Germany's and the world's most unusual cases of cold-blooded vampirism.

FACTS!

The population of the city of Nuremberg in 1972 was 514,976. By 2020, the population had barely changed and sat at 515,543.

Nuremberg is the second-largest city of the German state of Bavaria after its capital Munich.

The Nuremberg trials were held between November 20th 1945 and October 1st 1946. The trials were held after the Second World War by the Allies, against representatives of the defeated Nazi Germany.

The Bloodthirsty Harpe Brothers

Two men in search of a better future on the American frontier, became bloodthirsty criminals who claimed at least 39 lives, and in folklore are known as America's first serial killers.

The Harpe brothers, Micajah 'Big Harpe' and Wiley 'Little Harpe', are considered the first serial killers in the United States, active in the late 18th Century across Tennessee, Kentucky, Illinois, and Mississippi, leaving a blood-soaked trail of death – but their origins are relatively unknown.

It's widely thought the Harpe's were cousins or friends who travelled the Atlantic from Scotland, but they are more commonly known as brothers. It is also considered that their parents were born in Scotland and emigrated to America in search of a better life.

Some historians believe that the brother's accents, combined with the stories they told, and their allegiance to the British Crown, meant they were in fact born in Scotland. The truth is that the origins of the 'brothers' remain unknown.

However, despite their roots remaining slightly muddled, their crimes became folklore. By the end of their lives, they had killed at least 39 people between them but were suspected of having killed up to 50. Their crimes led to vigilante groups hunting them down across the four states.

Born in the 1760s, the Harpe's were raised in pro-British households and would grow up to remain loyal to the British Crown during the American Revolution. During the war, they became outlaws who began robbing and killing random people in and around the Appalachian Mountains.

Rape gang

In 1780, during the middle of the American Revolution, the Harpe's were taking advantage of the lawlessness the war had created and were said to have joined a rape gang in North Carolina. This meant they would roam the land in search of Patriot colonists and attack them.

In league with others in the gang, they would rape the women of the households, steal their possessions, murder their families, then burn and destroy their property. The Harpe's also took part in the kidnapping and rape of two teenage girls, with a third girl rescued by Captain James Wood of the continental army.

Wood's report would mention the Harpe brothers for the first time. Wood's brother, Frank Wood, a patriot soldier, claimed to have seen the Harpe's stealing from the dead on battlefields to pay their way through the country. During one of the battles, Frank attempted to kill Micajah but missed. The Harpe's were also seen during the Battle of Cowpens in 1781, in which 135 people were killed.

The Harpe's left North Carolina later that year following the British defeat at Yorktown, where 400 people were killed. They eloped with a band of Cherokee Indians to Tennessee, close to the Appalachian Mountains.

They joined the Cherokee's in various battles, fighting the Patriots to varying degrees of success. In the late 1780's, Frank Wood's younger sister, Susan, was kidnapped by the Harpe gang and forced to become Micajah's wife.

Over the next decade, the Harpe's lived in the village of Nickajack, in the foothills of the mountains, attempting to stay away from a life of crime and raising a number of children in the village. But in

1794, the village was attacked by American militia and the Harpe's escaped to Knoxville, Tennessee. Then three years later, in 1797, the Harpe's went on a crime spree that remains infamous to this day.

Rocks in the chest cavity

Both of the Harpe's wives had been forced into marriage and bore children to both men. It was widely reported that before the Harpe's eloped to Knoxville, they killed the infants in their sleep as their wives watched, before killing them too.

When in Knoxville, Wiley forced a minister's daughter, Sarah Rice, to marry him, while Micajah forced two sisters to be with him. All three were beaten and abused by the Harpe's and acted more like possessions than human beings.

The pair began stealing sheep and other cattle from their neighbours. They were caught and forced out of town by the locals but the Harpe's retaliated by killing the main witness, a man known as Johnson. His murder began an 18-month killing spree across the central states.

Many days later, Johnson's body was found on the banks of the Holstein River in Tennessee. His chest had been ripped open and his organs had been removed and replaced with rocks. Shockingly, the manner in which Johnson was killed and filled with rocks was something the Harpe's would do to many of their victims, and in essence, became their calling card.

Over the following weeks, they killed three travellers, stole goods from homes and acquired a horse from one of their victims. They made no real attempt to hide their victim's bodies and mostly left them in secluded areas of woodland or on riverbanks.

A month after the first murder, the Harpe's killed a traveller called John Langford who was foolishly wandering alone in the wilderness with a bag full of silver for prospecting. He too was ripped open and his chest cavity filled with stones and rocks – a murder which would lead to their first arrest.

River pirates

When lawmen realised the murders were connected and carried out by the Harpe's, they sent a posse after them. In no time at all, the Harpe's were captured and held in a jail in Danville, Kentucky. They managed to escape the next day and abandoned their three pregnant and abused wives in the town. But the wives and their infant children followed and joined them later on.

After their escape, the Harpe's had a $300 bounty placed on their heads, and so they made their way to Illinois, killing at least another five more people along the way, including a 13-year-old boy who was witness to one of their murders.

They then joined the infamous Samson Mason Gang in the stronghold of Cave-in-Rock, a gang known as river pirates, who raided merchant ships travelling along the Ohio River. It was with the gang that the Harpe's carried out some horrific murders, leading to the gang sending them on their way, as even they couldn't stomach what the Harpe's were doing.

Many of the river victims of the Harpe's were stripped naked, beaten, mutilated, then dragged behind a blindfolded horse which was led off the top of a cliff or over some rocks, killing them both. The Harpe's then travelled hundreds of miles on foot, claiming many more victims along the way.

In Logan County, Kentucky, they came across a young slave girl and her owners asleep at a camp. For whatever reason, the Harpe's slaughtered the entire family including the slave girl and left their bodies where they fell for others to find.

In addition, they killed a little girl after abducting her from a village, two more men who were found disembowelled, and a teenage boy who was found decapitated next to a large tree. Historians later suggested it was the wilderness of the frontier that allowed the Harpe's to get away with killing for so long.

Serial killers

In August 1799, Micajah snapped yet again and beat one of his wives to within an inch of her life because of her disobedience. He also became annoyed at their infant daughter for crying too loudly at the nightly camp and so he picked her up by her legs and smashed her head against a tree, killing her instantly.

They were given shelter by the Stegall family in Webster County, Kentucky, but they killed an overnight guest named William Love. Micajah had become upset that he had killed his own daughter for crying, and when he heard the Stegall's four-month-old boy doing the same, he cut the boy's throat before killing Mrs. Stegall.

When Mr. Moses Stegall returned home and saw what had happened, he formed a posse to track the Harpe's down. They caught up with Micajah first and surrounded him before shooting him in the back. Moses then took a blade and decapitated him, holding the head above his own, shouting to the high heavens that he had taken his revenge.

Wiley returned to Cave-in-Rock and sought shelter with the Samson Mason gang one last time and for the next three to four years, he was part of their gang. In around 1803, Wiley double-crossed Captain Mason, killed him, and took his head to town to claim the reward.

The authorities recognised Wiley from an old wanted poster and a vigilante group was raised. They chased him down, shot him, and executed him by hanging, before cutting his head off and displaying it on a stake to warn other outlaws.

His execution ended the reign of the Harpe brothers, who by that point were responsible for at least 39 murders across four states but suspected of at least 50. The unusual aspect of the Harpe brothers story, if not their sketchy origins, is that they killed with no real motive.

Some suggest they killed when they disagreed with or were angered by someone, while others conclude they killed simply to hide their tracks. Over the years, historians have attempted to trace the Harpe family roots, as their wives and surviving children went on to lead relatively normal lives but no record of them after 1820 has been found.

To go from the battlefields to beheading young boys, disembowelling victims like cattle, and brutally murdering infants, suggests there was more than just anger in the hearts of Big and Little Harpe, and that their infamy as America's first serial killers is more than well-founded.

FACTS!

The American Revolution was the United States' longest military conflict before the Vietnam War.

During the 18th Century, banishing criminals to the American colonies became the most common punishment by higher courts in Scotland.

In 2019, there were 40,647 violent crimes reported in the state of Tennessee, 498 were for murder.

Unthankful Brother Murdered with an Axe

A drunk man killed his brother with an axe as he slept because he forgot to say thank you for cooking dinner, in a cautionary tale where good manners mean the difference between life and death.

There are not many motives in true crime history where not being thanked has been the main instigator in a crime. But that's exactly what happened in the suburb of Wainuiomata, in the Wellington region of New Zealand's North Island.

A few months before the murder, 36-year-old New Zealander Fergus John Glen was living with his parents when his brother, 33-year-old Craig Glen, returned home after a messy split from his wife. It meant that Craig would be staying with them until things got sorted – which could have been forever.

Craig and his wife had three children together and the children were not allowed to see him during the separation which caused friction between him and his family. Over the following weeks, Craig and Fergus squabbled over the littlest thing and their arguments would occasionally end in physical fights.

Despite their fighting, they always made up the day after and attempted to live alongside each other, for their parents sakes, who never expected their children to still be living with them in the thirties. On occasion, Fergus would make the evening meal which was exactly what he did on 7th March 2003.

The family sat down for dinner and chomped away before having some alcoholic drinks from the fridge. All was going well until Craig forgot to thank Fergus for cooking the dinner but Fergus didn't say anything, instead resorting to sitting alone, drinking, and getting angrier by the minute.

Axeman in the night

Fergus hid his growing anger by drinking whisky and watching TV and was left internally fuming when Craig went to bed without saying anything to him. According to his parents, Fergus was in a jovial mood, which goes to show how much someone can hide their emotions on the inside.

As his parents turned in for the night, the mask protecting Fergus from the world dropped and he realised what he needed to do to resolve the issue that had been fermenting in his mind. He drunkenly stumbled into the basement and selected the best axe for the job.

Then he traipsed upstairs holding the axe to his side before standing in the open doorway of the room his brother was sleeping in. Fergus remembers standing in the doorway for a few moments before his anger got the better of him and he stepped inside.

As it was dark, he could only tell where his brother's head was by the light from the hallway behind him. He raised the axe over his shoulder and brought it down on Craig's head. He then hit him another seven times in the head, neck and face, splattering blood all over the room and himself.

His mother was awoken by the sound of heavy thudding, as if someone was chopping wood but it didn't make sense to her as it was in the middle of the night. Fergus calmly walked downstairs and put the axe back in the basement.

As he was coming back into the living room, his mother was on the stairs wondering what the hell was going on. Fergus, covered in blood, nodded and said, 'I've done him, with an axe.' His mother ran upstairs to Craig's room and screamed the house down.

Bloodbath

Fergus didn't try and stop his parents calling police, he claimed he knew what he had done and would receive his punishment. When police arrived in the early hours of the morning, they were met with a bloodbath.

Fergus told police that Craig had annoyed him by not saying thank you and that he wasn't proud of the murder but he did it anyway. A forensic examination of the body concluded that almost all of Craig's blood had exited his body.

The blows from the axe had severed the upper spine and virtually decapitated Craig. The medical examiner's office confirmed that Craig would not have felt a thing as the first one or two blows would have rendered him unconscious.

Fergus pleaded guilty to murder in late 2003 and was ultimately sentenced to life in prison with a minimum tariff of ten years. Despite becoming eligible for parole in 2013, his first hearing was in 2016 where he was denied parole, and again in 2017.

From 2017 to 2019, Fergus was placed in a self-care facility, with plans to reintegrate him into society. He also had psychological treatment and had been working outside the facility among the public. Then in late 2019, Fergus was granted parole on license and his elderly mother was there to meet him.

In this unusual murder, it was clear, even by Fergus's own words, that alcohol played a huge part in his adverse decision to end the life of his brother in such a manner. But Fergus was rightfully punished to the maximum extent of the law as he had taken away a father from three of his children, despite the excuse behind it.

That Fergus will forever live with the knowledge he killed his own brother, is perhaps punishment enough beyond his sentence. But the next time you forget to thank someone for cooking your food or doing anything for you, then it's probably best to remember the tale of Craig and Fergus Glen, where good manners could mean the difference between life and death.

FACTS!

There is no category for murder caused by an axe in general crime statistics. Murders caused by an axe are bundled under knife-related violence or sharp objects.

Using the Global Peace Index of 2021, New Zealand is considered the second safest country in the world, second only to Iceland.

New Zealand Police is divided into 12 districts, 9 in the North Island and 3 in the South. Each district is divided into areas and has a central station from which subsidiary and suburban stations are managed.

The Serpent

An unusual serial killer and lifetime criminal, who claimed the lives of dozens of western tourists travelling the hippie trail, killing to cover his tracks and live off the proceeds of his victims.

Serial killers generally kill because of three main reasons; pleasure, criminal enterprise, or psychological. Charles Sobhraj falls under the category of criminal enterprise, which means he killed for either financial gain, drugs, gang-related killings, or organised crime.

Robbery, insurance scams, and welfare fraud are some of the ways that one might benefit financially from a murder. Sobhraj was part of the 1970s and 1980s serial killer epidemic, where serial killing was at its peak.

This was down to numerous factors including the after-effects of World War Two, attitudes towards women in the late 1960s and 1970s, the creation of highways which allowed killers to move around more freely, along with the fall-out of the Vietnam War, among many other reasons.

Sobhraj was born in Saigon in 1944 to a Vietnamese mother and Indian father. His international life began early when his parents divorced shortly after his birth. He was adopted by his mother's new boyfriend, a French Army lieutenant, and they travelled between South-East Asia and France on many occasions.

He became a French national because of the adoption and held a French passport for most of his life, offering more opportunity that a Vietnamese passport at the time. Due to his scattered upbringing and neglect, he became a petty thief and small-time criminal before his first arrest in 1963, when he was 19-years-old.

While serving his first short jail sentence in Paris, he met one of France's high society rich kids named Felix d'Escogne, who was working as a prison volunteer.

Sobhraj moved in with Felix when he was released a few months later. He then managed to flitter between high society and the criminal world with ease. Though Sobhraj is known as The Serpent, chameleon would have been more appropriate.

The hippie trail

In the late 1960s, Sobhraj was arrested for driving a stolen vehicle, and sentenced to another eight months in jail before he married a high-society French girl name Chantal Compagnon. In 1970, he left France before he could be arrested on another charge, and ended up in Mumbai, India.

He began a car theft and smuggling operation and used the profits for his new gambling addiction. In 1973 he was arrested and held on an armed robbery charge in Delhi, but with the help of his new wife, he managed to escape. Despite a recapture, he was bailed out and then eloped to Kabul, Afghanistan.

In Kabul, he was arrested again for robbing tourists on the hippie trail and again managed to escape. His wife and newly born child left him and returned to Paris. From 1973 to 1975 with help from his half-brother, they travelled through many countries across Europe and the Middle East, robbing tourists and involving themselves in criminal activity.

They were arrested in Athens, Greece, where Sobhraj managed to escape yet again. His half-brother was sentenced to 18-years in prison. All of the above was before he even killed his first victim; a Seattle-based female who threatened to expose Sobhraj's criminal activities in 1975.

She was found drowned in the surf of a tidal pool in the Gulf of Thailand, wearing only her bikini. In the same year, Sobhraj burned to death a young man named Vitali Hakim, near the Pattaya resort, and also strangled to death a young couple who he feared would expose his criminal activities.

The Bikini Killer

Again in the same year, Sobhraj killed Hakim's girlfriend who had travelled to Thailand to look for him. She was found face down in the surf, wearing a similar style-bikini to the first victim. This is how he got the additional moniker of the Bikini Killer.

At the time, Sobhraj had recruited an Indian helper named Ajay Chowdhary, who was known to have assisted Sobhraj in his crimes. Shockingly, no trace of Chowdhary has ever been found but it is suspected Sobhraj may have killed him too.

Sobhraj had a charming but manipulative personality and people were drawn to him, in the same way that Charles Manson was able to recruit followers. Also in the same way that the likes of Ted Bundy and Rodney Alcala were able to charm and manipulate everyone around them.

He would gain the trust of foreign backpackers, mostly from Europe and the United States, then poison them before nurturing them back to health. He did this to gain control over them and ensure their trust in him, as the victims didn't know they were being poisoned.

In December of 1975, he eloped to Nepal and killed two more backpackers and used their passports to head back to Thailand. This was an era where travel between countries was a lot easier and restrictions were minimal, especially in Southeast Asia and the Middle East.

Sobhraj was most likely the reason our parents told us never to go backpacking to Southeast Asia, or travel to countries that were not English-speaking. Around the same time, stories of murdered backpackers and missing travellers were appearing in newspapers across the UK, America, and Europe.

Though Sobhraj wasn't responsible for all of them, it did paint a dire picture of Southeast Asia specifically. His last victims were a group of four French students travelling through New Delhi, he tricked them into becoming a tour guide for them. As they were being poisoned, three of them realised what was happening and managed to overpower Sobhraj before the police arrived to arrest him.

The prison years

Sobhraj was sentenced to twelve years in an Indian prison but the story doesn't end there. Ten years later, he realised that if he was to be released, then an outstanding Thai warrant would ensure his extradition to the country where the death penalty would have been handed out.

At the time, Thai warrants had an expiration time of 20 years which meant Sobhraj needed to remain in prison for another ten years instead of being released to Thai authorities. Inside the Indian prison, Sobhraj was living a life of luxury, having learned quickly how to bribe the guards and other prisoners.

In 1986, he put on a lavish party for the guards but secretly poisoned them and then calmly walked out the jail. He travelled south to Goa and patiently waited his recapture. When he was rearrested, he was given an additional ten years on his sentence – exactly what he wanted.

In February 1997, the then 52-year-old Sobhraj was released and allowed to return to France. In the six years that followed, he was paid to be interviewed by researchers and movie producers. One investigator claimed that Sobhraj had received $15million USD for the movie rights to his story.

This is something that wouldn't be allowed to happen nowadays, at least in the UK and United States. In 1978 in the U.S., the Son of Sam Law was passed after David Berkowitz came close to making money off his story.

This law went some way to setting the standard for similar laws throughout the United States and some other countries. Dennis Nilsen was allowed to publish his autobiography but shortly after, the British government banned it and implemented a similar law.

In 2003, Sobhraj was spotted in Kathmandu, Nepal, and was reported to Nepalese authorities as there was an outstanding warrant in the country without the time limit that Thailand had. He was arrested and sentenced to life a year later.

Since then, he's married a Nepalese woman, Nihita Biswas, while in jail in 2008. Nihita went on to be part of the Indian version of Big Brother in 2011. She remains married to him and claims her husband has not killed anyone or been charged with murder.

Except, he did kill and he has been charged – and convicted.

In 2010, he was sentenced to life in a new trial for the murder of Canadian backpacker Connie Jo Bronzich. In 2014, he was sentenced to life again for the murder of another Canadian traveller. Despite being seriously ill in recent years, he remains alive in his prison cell, in Nepal.

Criminal enterprise

Sobhraj killed to protect his crimes from being exposed and those who stood in his way. He never killed out of sexual pleasure or to sate a desire for death. He killed for passports and papers that allowed him to move freely between multiple countries. Yet, he is still a serial killer.

Criminal enterprise is as dangerous as sexual or psychological reasons. Sobhraj later stated in an interview that he killed purely out of business interest and saw it as a job to give him access to the means that allowed his criminal activities to continue.

It has been confirmed that in his formative years, he suffered neglect at the hands of his mother's French boyfriend and the constant moving between different countries had a negative effect on his psychological growth.

Sobhraj fell into the trap of wanting to live a high society life but doing so in an illegal fashion. He had been manipulating people since he was a youngster by getting other children to steal for him. His mother also blamed him for her separation from his father, which tied into the abandonment he would have felt from the boyfriend.

The feeling of constantly being on the run and not having a home to settle into can see someone prefer to live in the criminal world with little respect for morals or the lives of others. He was able to exploit the weaknesses of people all around him. According to those who knew him, he had a small conscience, if any at all, and lived on impulses and calculated aggression.

Bizarre paradox

Had Sobhraj been convicted in Thailand for the crimes he committed then he would have been executed long before now. Let's not make the mistake of thinking he has ever been someone's friend. He's used people for his own gain, all of his life, and it doesn't change with age.

Some people refer to him as a serial killer celebrity but you won't be seeing Sobhraj on the likes of I'm A Celebrity, Get Me Out Of Here, any time soon. That would be a whole different kind of show. Confessions and interviews with killers are mostly readily available after conviction so the information is already there for easy consumption.

On the one hand, people have a macabre fascination with all things relating to serial killers. On the other hand, the public don't really want to see them get rich off the back of their crimes. It's a bizarre paradox where both sides are hungry but we are able to sate our hunger in the same way serial killers sate theirs.

Fame then, surely is inevitable, as we strive to know more about those who commit the worse type of crimes. Serial killers are not criminal masterminds, they are people of circumstance and opportunity, moulded through nurture, not nature. Sobhraj should not be held in high esteem but his story should be told, so that we can understand why and indeed how those like him do the things they do.

FACTS!

The Hippie Trail is a journey that started in Western Europe and crossed through the Balkans, the Middle East and Southeast Asia.

While in London, Sobhraj supposedly met with the then editor of The Spectator and future British Prime Minister Boris Johnson.

Sobhraj claimed he worked for the CIA and that they abandoned him when he was arrested in Nepal in 2003.

Tattingstone Suitcase Murder

A young man disappeared in London only to turn up dead ten days later, chopped up into eight pieces and left in two suitcases on a Suffolk farm, leading to a half-century long investigation.

Muswell Hill in North London is already known to the true crime community as the location where British serial killer Dennis Nilsen claimed many of his victims in the early 1980s. But over a decade earlier in 1967, a young man went missing from Muswell Hill, only to be found later chopped up into eight pieces and left in two suitcases.

17-year-old Bernard Oliver was born in 1950 and lived in North London with his family in Muswell Hill. From a young age, he was known to have learning difficulties and attended a special needs school to help him through education. He was known to look younger than his age and had moles on his face.

He was the fourth of six children, with four brothers and one sister. A year before the murder, Bernard's parents had separated which placed a lot of stress on him and his siblings. He left school and got a paid job at a local warehouse, packing goods.

On Friday 6th January 1967, Bernard spent the evening with friends in Muswell Hill before parting ways to head home for the weekend. He disappeared on the way back and never made it home, but at the time it wasn't abnormal as Bernard sometimes spent the entire night out with friends.

As Saturday morning came around, his family became concerned and contacted police who were unable to find any evidence as to where he might be. For the next ten days, he was listed as a missing person but his family knew something bad must have happened as he wouldn't stay out all weekend.

On 16th January, a farm worker, Fred Burggy, was attending to routine work on his farm in Tattingstone,

Suffolk, almost 80 miles away from Muswell Hill, when he stumbled across two heavy suitcases. Inside, he found the dismembered remains of a young man.

Head in the press

Police arrived on the scene and cordoned off most of the farm but they were unable to identify the victim due to the condition of the remains. They took the unusual decision to release the image of the victim's head to the press.

They instructed a funeral worker to clean and dress the decapitated head, prop the eyes up, and redo the hair, in order to make it eligible to be used in newspapers. When editors at various newspapers received the press release, many refused to print it – but some did, leading to the identification.

The following day, 80 miles away in London, Chris Oliver, Bernard's brother, and a friend, were waiting for a bus when they saw the newspapers in the local newsagents window. Chris's friend nudged him and pointed at the window, informing him that his brother was in the papers.

Before even reading the story, all Chris saw was the headline that read, 'Suitcase Murder.' Chris told his family who then informed the police. In the days before bereavement support, the police put all members of the Oliver family down as suspects before removing them when there was no evidence to suggest they had killed one of their own.

During the autopsy of the remains, it was concluded that Bernard had been killed approximately two days before the discovery of the suitcases, meaning he had been held captive for over a week. It was also determined he had been brutally raped.

Red herring

When the press named Bernard, police began to get calls from across North London and Suffolk, from witnesses who believed they had seen him. Some of the witness statements claimed to have seen Bernard around Muswell Hill after he disappeared but they were put down to seeing his brothers instead.

In Tattingstone, a local resident saw a middle-aged man wearing a long dark trench coat and trilby hat carrying a suitcase a couple of days before the discovery. She wasn't able to identify him further but is has long been suspected he was involved in the murder.

Two physical pieces of evidence were taking from the cases. One of the cases had the initials 'P.V.A' written on the inside, and a hand towel recovered from the other case bore the laundry mark of 'QL 42'.

A matchbox found in the pocket of Bernard's coat were from a brand of matches that were usually marketed and sold in Israel. Having cut up the body to such an extent, it seemed unusual that the killer would leave physical pieces of evidence such as a towel or matchbox, unless it was a deliberate diversion – a red herring.

Bernard's nails had been cut by the killer and his hair had been freshly trimmed. His stomach contents revealed that he had recently eaten a meal which meant his captor or captors had been keeping him alive.

The investigation went cold quickly but a freedom of information act request in 2000 revealed that the prime suspects were two medical doctors, John Byles and Martin Reddington. Byles was said to be part of the infamous Holy Trinity paedophile ring.

Holy Trinity

Byles was found dead in his bedroom at the Prince of Wales Hotel in Proserpine, Australia on 19th January 1975. At the time of his death, he was wanted for extradition back to the United Kingdom for his involvement in the Holy Trinity ring.

Byles was a doctor at a south London surgery who was accused of persuading young boys to take part in sexual acts after plying them with alcohol. He took many photos of his sexual interactions that he then sold to child pornographers in Denmark and the Netherlands.

The Holy Trinity ring were a group of professionals who stood trial in 1975 at Leeds Crown Court and were found guilty of the sexual abuse of young boys, and involvement in the production of child pornography. Some of the incidents took place at the Holy Trinity Church in Huddersfield, where boys were abused in the crypt and at the altar.

Reverend John Poole, childcare worker Raymond Varley, and teacher Clive Wilcock were convicted of their crimes and sentenced to various prison terms. Byles was named as one of the accused and the trial went ahead without him as the authorities were trying to track him down in Australia.

It was suspected he died by suicide but there have been no records of the cause of death ever released.

The Holy Trinity case only came to light recently due to the passage of time. Which makes one wonder how many more similar cases were hidden from the public eye.

Evil men

Suffolk police were informed of Byles's death and closed their case on him. The investigation was aware that Byles had admitted to a colleague that he murdered a cabin boy and cut up his body, though why he freely offered that information is anyone's guess. His suicide note simply apologised for his actions but he never made it clear what exactly he was apologising for.

Martin Reddington was a colleague of Byles and once had a surgery in Muswell Hill. Two years before Bernard's murder, an arrest warrant was issued due to allegations of rape against young males in 1965. Before capture, he fled to South Africa but was known to make many return trips to the UK under a pseudonym.

Reddington and Byles would have casual sex with each other whenever they met and their fantasies about abusing young boys only grew. Though Reddington wasn't said to be part of the Holy Trinity ring, it was suspected he reaped the proceeds from them by way of images.

He moved to Australia shortly after Byles's death and in 1977 was charged with sexually assaulting a young male. While the British authorities were still investigating him, Reddington died in May 1995, aged 63, taking any secrets he had to the grave.

Both Byles and Reddington were described as evil men who instigated much of the abuse against young boys. It has also long been suspected that one or both were involved in Bernard's abduction and murder. But as much as the evidence seems to point at Byles and Reddington, there were other suspects that have never been discounted – including none other than Reggie Kray.

A rare killer

Gangster, Reginald Kray, was sentenced to life in 1969 with his brother Ronnie, for two murders, along with gang related crimes. After his death, a former cellmate spoke to the press and claimed that Reggie had confessed to the murder of a young gay boy.

Though the boy in question was thought to be the disappearance of Edward Smith in 1967, one of the Kray's properties was only 16 miles away from Tattingstone. However, Bernard had no reason to be involved with the Kray's, unless Ronnie – who was bisexual – was involved with him sexually.

Another suspect was record producer Joe Meek who had once employed the young Bernard as a tape-stacker in his studio. He was convicted in 1963 of engaging in lewd acts with other men in public toilets. He went on to kill his landlady in 1967 before taking his own life.

Another music industry man, Australian DJ Tony Windsor was suspected by police as he worked on board the MV Galaxy, a pirate radio ship that was harboured 12 miles away from Tattingstone at the time of the disappearance and murder. Windsor was close friends with Meek, was gay, had an alcohol problem and was known to touch young boys.

As the decades went on and the case continued to be unsolved, it seemed more likely that Bernard became a victim of either Byles, Reddington, or the Holy Trinity ring. Though he was 17, Bernard was child-like in stature and mental capacity.

It is though incredibly unusual and rare for a victim of a killer to be placed in two suitcases side by side. Usually, in cases like this, the body parts are spread over a wide area to hide evidence and the location of the kill. It remains bizarre for the killer to have left the cases on the farm to be found.

Profilers have since drawn up a report suggesting the killer or killers were likely living in or near Tattingstone at the time, as Bernard would have been killed close to the farm. The initials on the case and on the towel were suspected to have been planted by the killer and were red herrings.

The investigation has been reopened many times, with the last cold case crew looking at the case in 2015. To this day, Bernard's murder remains unsolved and as bizarre as ever. As time progresses, it seems more unlikely that the true suspect will be named – but we hold out in hope.

FACTS!

The village of Tattingstone has a population of 540, while its county, Suffolk, has a population of 758,000.

The village was split into two halves in the 1970s when the valley was flooded to make a 400-acre reservoir.

Raymond Varley, who was convicted in the Holy Trinity case, was wanted by Indian authorities in connection with his involvement in child abuse in Goa.

The Death of Kirsty MacColl

Famed for duetting the Christmas song, Fairytale of New York, Kirsty died in a suspicious boating accident, leading her family to believe there was a cover up to protect the real culprit.

There are many Christmas songs that have stood the test of time and are found on almost every Christmas compilation out there. But perhaps none more divisive than 'Fairytale of New York', a Christmas song by The Pogues, on which British singer Kirsty MacColl lent her voice to.

Some love it, some hate it, but when Christmas time comes around, you'll be sure to hear it blaring from shop speaker systems. MacColl was born in England in 1959 to Scottish parents and grew up in Croydon, South London, where she found a love of all things music.

She was the daughter of folk singer, Ewan MacColl, who was part of the 1960s folk music revival. As such, she grew up around music and sang on various folk and punk songs around at the time, including an EP from punk band 'Drug Addix', who were managed by Chiswick Records.

The band was her segue into a solo career and she was ultimately signed to the German-British record label Polydor Records in 1981. Her career moved from backing vocals to writing her own songs and other artist's songs, before returning as a backing vocalist for some of the world's most famous singers.

These included backing vocals on songs by Robert Plant, Alison Moyet, Simple Minds and Talking Heads, before she hit the big time with Fairytale of New York in 1987, duetting with The Pogues singer Shane MacGowan.

Just 13 years later, and with her career going from strength to strength, 41-year-old Kirsty died in a suspicious boating accident in Mexico. The deckhand who was allegedly in control of the boat was found guilty of culpable homicide – except he wasn't on the boat at the time of Kirsty's death.

Diving holiday

In December 2000, Kirsty was in Cuba presenting a radio show for the BBC. When her short contract ended, she decided to make the most of her stay in Latin America and took her sons, Jamie, 15, and Louis, 13, on holiday to the island of Cozumel, twelve miles off the Yucatan Peninsula in Mexico.

It was a long overdue break as Kirsty had been working for the previous 18 months non-stop and was looking forward to taking time off with her family. And there was no better place than Cozumel, as one of her passions was diving and she was ready to show her sons exactly what all the fuss was about.

On 18th December, Kirsty and her sons were scuba diving at the Chankanaab reef, which is part of the National Marine Park of Cozumel, one of the most richly diverse ecosystems on the planet, when tragedy struck.

The original reports stated that Kirsty and her children were diving in a designated diving area with a divemaster and trainer named Ivan Diaz. When the group resurfaced from a short dive, a powerboat was coming towards them at high speed.

Kirsty apparently saw the boat coming at them and pushed her sons out the way but the boat smashed into her, causing massive head and chest injuries, which killed her instantly. Diaz radioed for help, and

Kirsty's lifeless body was taken to the shoreline, where the authorities were waiting.

Her family in the UK were informed of her death and were told it was an unavoidable and freak accident. But as the family watched the news and were told different versions of the death by eyewitnesses, they began to believe that something untoward had happened.

Swimming in blood

For many members of the public, the loss of Kirsty was a dark day in the music world, and her body was flown back to the United Kingdom where she was cremated at a large ceremony in Kew, London, not too far from her family home.

But beyond the outpouring of grief, and behind the headlines, lay a cover-up story that was about to be exposed. The person allegedly in control of the boat was Mexican supermarket millionaire tycoon, Guillermo González Nova.

The owner of the boat was Nova's brother, who was the founder of the supermarket chain, who wasn't on the boat at the time. Nova was on board the boat with other members of his family and told the authorities and resulting investigation that he was travelling at only one knot and was not inside the designated diving zone.

Local television in Mexico showed Nova being led away for questioning, and there was no doubt in their mind that Nova was in control of the boat. The next day, Nova was freed because 26-year-old deckhand

José Cen Yam, who was employed by Nova, came forward and admitted to killing Kirsty.

He claimed he was in control of the boat at the time, despite not having a license to drive such a powerful boat. He reiterated Nova's story and said the boat was travelling at one knot and that there were no other boats in the direction they were going and again that they were not near the designated diving zone and were in fact headed out towards the sea, away from the shore.

For Jean Newlove, Kirsty's mother, things were not adding up. When her grandsons returned home from Mexico without their mother, they told her that they had come up from a dive in the diving zone, where they were with their instructor, Diaz.

Almost immediately, the powerboat was flying towards them. Louis later said that his mother pushed him out of the way, with the boat barely missing his head. As the propellers shot over his head, he found himself swimming in his mother's blood, such was the impact from the hit – which raised many questions.

The fall guy

Cen Yam claimed he was going at a speed of one knot but the injuries caused to Kirsty were consistent with a boat travelling at 30 times that speed. The boat stopped over 300 feet away, and only did so when the person in control realised the propeller had been damaged.

Two autopsies were carried out on the body, one in Mexico that claimed she had died from simple head injuries, and one in London, where the doctor concluded she had been virtually cut in half from the impact of the boat. Her left leg and chest were almost severed completely through. A boat travelling at one knot was unlikely to have caused the damage seen.

Joan later heard from witnesses that the paramedics vomited when they saw the body. Eyewitnesses to the incident, including diving expert Diaz, claimed that Cen Yam was not at the controls and that the boat was travelling way beyond the speed of one knot.

Despite evidence and witness statements to the contrary, Cen Yam was sent to trial and charged with culpable homicide, a charge that involves the illegal killing of a person either with or without an intention to kill depending upon how a particular jurisdiction has defined the offence.

Cen Yam was found guilty and sentenced to almost three years in prison but because the offence had been committed in Mexico, he was allowed to pay a fine instead of going to jail – the massive amount of $63 USD (1,000 pesos).

Protecting the Nova family

He was also ordered to pay a little over $2,000 to Kirsty's family, which he did with ease, despite his low-paid job as a deckhand. Years after the incident, friends of Cen Yam began to recount stories that he had been paid a large amount of money to take the fall for the death.

The pay-off was said to have come from none other than the wealthy Nova family. This led to Kirsty's family starting a campaign called '*Justice For Kirsty*', or JFK for short. They instructed lawyers to campaign for a judicial review into the events surrounding Kirsty's death, believing evidence was being hidden.

Kirsty's insurance providers and private detectives began digging into the facts of the case and found a succession of conflicting statements and incorrect claims. It appeared that the Mexican authorities were covering up much of the evidence, especially in relation to Nova.

In May 2006, Cozumel federal prosecutor Emilio Cortez Ramírez was found liable for a breach of authority in his handling of the case and was ordered to step down. For Mexican authorities, the case was closed, the death was classed as culpable homicide, the suspect was convicted, and a leading official resigned.

Mexico refused to cooperate with the JFK group or their lawyers beyond 2006. The truth is that Kirsty suffered a horrific death that could have been avoided, had proper maritime rules been followed in terms of speed and adhering to the diving zone.

Cen Yam took the fall, as the wealthy Nova family could not have one of their own up on a homicide charge, culpable or not. If it had been proven that the boat was travelling over one knot and was inside the diving zone, then Nova could have been sentenced to life in prison.

Bombshell

At the time, Mexico was – and still is – one of the most corrupt countries in the world. All it would have taken was for Nova to bribe the officials and pay off Cen Yam to take the fall, for the situation to be resolved.

Diaz, who was in charge of the dive, later provided his own story to the JFK campaign, that he and the MacColl's had been out of the water for almost half a minute, before the boat which was a few hundred metres away, turned and sped straight towards them.

He believed it would turn at the last minute, as they were in plain sight, but the boat continued to gain speed and slammed into Kirsty, dragging her under the propeller. Diaz's claim was backed up by the captains of three other boats in the area.

He also dropped the bombshell that it was Nova's teenage sons who were in control of the boat and not Nova himself, which could have been why Nova was so keen for someone else to take the blame. Ever since the incident, locals on the island refuse to speak about it, out of fear of the power that the Nova family still hold over their way of life.

Jean and the JFK group stopped campaigning in 2009, the year that Carlos González Nova died of natural causes. They handed off the campaign's funds to two music charities, one based in Mexico, and the other in Cuba, believing that Kirsty herself would have approved.

What is clear is that Kirsty saved her sons lives by pushing them out of the way of the boat, in what could have been a larger tragedy. Her legacy continues to this day and her contribution to the world of music is heard every year around Christmas time.

FACTS!

'Fairytale of New York' never reached number one on the UK singles charts but has sold over 1.25million copies in the country.

Comercial Mexicana, the supermarket chain owned by the Nova family, is the third largest supermarket chain in Mexico, and was originally called La Comer.

The island of Cozumel is home to 100,000 residents, and tourism is the main economy on the island.

The Blackburn Cult

Also known as the Great Eleven, the Blackburn Cult included strange rituals, animal sacrifice, the attempted resurrection of a teenage princess, and a con by two failed actresses.

Known to her followers as Queen May or the Heel of God, failed actress May Otis Blackburn was the leader of a cult called Divine Order of the Royal Arms of the Great Eleven, or the Great Eleven or Blackburn Cult for short.

It was one of the stranger cults to come out of early 20th Century Los Angeles. May founded the group in 1922, aged 60, in the neighbourhood of Bunker Hill and would later set up a retreat on the outskirts of the city of Simi Valley in Southern California.

May's 24-year-old daughter, Ruth Wieland Rizzio, helped her set up the cult. Ruth was a wannabe actress and songwriter who had minimal success but failed to take leaps big enough to have seen her love of entertainment transfer to a career. May also failed in getting any acting jobs.

Due to their passion for acting, the family, including May's husband and Ruth's stepbrother, Ward Blackburn, moved to Bunker Hill from Oregon, as Hollywood was only six miles away from the neighbourhood, in the hope that the women's careers might take off.

When she couldn't get any acting jobs, Ruth took on a position as a taxi dancer, which is a long-dead position of someone who dances with a partner for money. Single males in clubs would buy a dance ticket and present that ticket to a female who would cash it in and dance with them for one song. It's no wonder it went out of fashion.

In 1922, May and Ruth went to the press and told them an unusual story. One night, while they were resting in their apartment, the angels Gabriel and

Michael appeared and proclaimed them to be the two witnesses from a vision in the Book of Revelation.

Simi Valley retreat

May claimed the two angels would be dictating books to them that revealed the secrets of the Universe, the mysteries of Heaven, and the meaning of life and death. To top it all off, the angels would also be revealing an apocalyptic event that would occur on earth after the Seventh Seal in Heaven had been broken, following completion of the first book.

The revelation to the press also coincided with the time that the family were beginning to come under immense financial pressure due to lack of work. But the Blackburn's had their work cut out for them, as California in the 1920s was experiencing a surge of cults and cult-like groups.

In May 1924, Ruth married a work friend named Sam Rizzio, who moved into her home which had become ground zero for the cult. Realising how forceful the cult was, Sam begged Ruth to leave, which caused a fight. He allegedly hit Ruth and her followers turned on him. Bizarrely, Sam was never seen again, dead or alive.

Somehow, the angel story managed to convince many others to join in their beliefs, and by 1924, the newly proclaimed Divine Order of the Royal Arms of the Great Eleven, moved to a large site in Simi Valley, where members and financiers of the cult built houses and tended to the land. Coincidentally timed directly after Sam disappeared.

Many followers worked at tomato packing plants, helping fund the cult as they awaited May and Ruth to complete their succession of books, written by the angels themselves, and mostly funded by donations from the followers. The first book was to be called The Great Sixth Seal and would share prophecies and interpretations of the Universe.

It would also bizarrely point to untapped oil deposits around the world, something that attracted investors to May's way of life. By promising to tell investors where untapped oil reserves were, she could bring in more money to fund their way of life.

A businessman and oil company owner named Clifford Dabney invested $40,000 (worth $800,000 today) into the Blackburn Cult, on the basis that the angels would reveal to May the location of the oil reserves. Dabney also offered more money if the locations turned out to be correct. He was also part of the reason why the cult were able to afford the area of land in Simi Valley.

Ritual of corpses

Dabney gave May money on the premise that she would give him the locations before the book was printed. Unsurprisingly, she never did, but Dabney's involvement in the cult would ultimately bring the entire thing crashing down.

Before that happened, the Blackburn Cult were involved in particularly unsavoury actions. Curiously, the Simi Valley retreat was only a few miles away from where Charles Manson would set up shop 40 years later.

May was said to have taken much of her cult visions from the worship of the ancient Greek goddess

Hecate, who was the goddess of night and sorcery. Somehow, she managed to convince her followers that Hecate was also speaking to her.

In early 1925, one of their young followers, 16-year-old Willa Rhoads, whose parents had brought her into the cult, died after a tooth infection, which had never been treated. Her death was never reported because May and Ruth decided they might be able to resurrect an ancient princess inside of Willa's body.

They wrapped the body in spices and salts to preserve her as much as possible, then buried her under the floorboards of the Rhoads's cabin at the reserve. The ritual to resurrect the unnamed princess involved the sacrifice of seven dogs, and their corpses were buried around Willa's tomb in a perfect circle.

The seven dogs were meant to represent the seven major tones of Gabriel's trumpet, as described by Gabriel to May. It has long been unclear if Willa died of natural causes or if May or Ruth killed her in order to practice a ritual they knew wouldn't work but which would strengthen their position with their followers.

Devil's Hole

In 1928, while awaiting the final chapters from the angels, the cult went in three cars on a 500-mile spiritual trip to the Death Valley National Park and stopped at a location called the Devil's Hole, a geothermal pool and cavern.

May convinced her followers the Devil's Hole was the entrance to a hidden world but was known to be a place where murder victims were sometimes dumped.

Charles Manson also used the Devil's Hole to discard of some of his cult's personal items, with some suggesting bodies also.

The night they arrived, forest rangers saw a fire at the Devil's Hole and went in for a closer look but watched from afar. The followers were sat on the ground looking up at their high priestesses in long purple robes. They sacrificed two mules, who they called the Jaws of Death, and cut their throats before pushing their bodies into the well.

Following the sacrifice, the rangers watched with some trepidation as all members of the cult took their clothes off and danced naked around the fire, with some taking part in sexual activities as others watched.

The cause of the fire was a hastily constructed oven where 30-year-old follower Florence Turner was being slowly burned. May claimed that the fire would cure her blood disorder but Florence died of her injuries two days later.

After the group returned to Simi Valley, many were starting to think that May and Ruth were making the whole thing up but didn't want to say anything in front of the others. However, Clifford Dabney was already waiting to turn the tables.

Origin of God

Six months later in 1929, May and Ruth were arrested on theft charges, instigated by Dabney. At the same time, many of the followers disbanded and brought their own charges of theft and deception against the two self-proclaimed high priestesses.

Newspaper reports at the time refer to May as a cult leader and that she referred to herself as the Heel of God. May was charged with 12 counts of theft but the investigation had led to the tale of the 16-year-old girl and the burning of Florence.

Despite investigating thoroughly, the LAPD could not find any evidence of wrongdoing, and May got off from what could have been a manslaughter charge in the case of Florence. For fraud and theft, she was sentenced to 12 years in prison but released 18 months later when she won an appeal in the Supreme Court.

She was released on the basis that, *'this is a free country, where there is freedom of religious worship, and it is not actionable to the court if the defendant made certain representations as to being divine.'* Meaning it was not deemed theft because May believed she was a conduit for the angels.

But by that point, the cult had disbanded and the Divine Order of the Royal Arms of the Great Eleven was no more. Ruth and May tried to re-establish the group in Lake Tahoe but to no avail. The 'Great Sixth Seal' book was never completed and never published.

Followers who had access to the draft of the book would later claim it was just a muddled mess of obscure references and minimal knowledge. In 1936, May published a book called 'The Origin of God' under DeVross & Company, who are still active in the publishing world to this day.

The book opens with *'the revelation given in this book on the origin of God and creation, was revealed to the author from immortal authority, and the author is convinced of its facts and truths.*' But no one else was convinced and the book sold only a handful of copies.

May writes about God being bread and describes bread diets in great detail for some reason, she claims the Universe is measured in spiritual calculation, repeats entire paragraphs, says space has four opposing winds, invisible forces, and that her nose – not space – can smell flowers from a distance.

Dion Fortune, she was not, but May Blackburn did have an impact on cults in early 20th Century California, so much so that Charles Manson would often refer to her. Ruth vanished into obscurity, and May died shortly after the book was published, supposedly to be with the angels.

FACTS!

The Book of Revelation is the final book of the New Testament and is known as an apocalyptic book. The author of the Book of Revelation is known only as John.

In the Book of Revelation, the two witnesses are two prophets who are never identified, which is why so many alternative religious orders are led by those claiming to be one of the prophets.

There were hundreds of cults that began in Los Angeles in the 1920s, and many have been lost to the annals of history. They formed what was known as the new religious movement of California.

The Tall Tale of Toby Cole

A deaf mute teenage girl stumbled into a school having escaped a satanic cult, but there was something about her story that didn't add up, leading to an extraordinary revelation.

Satanic panic had firmly set in during the 1980s, media were portraying horror stories of cults and rituals, and films had begun to capitalise on the wave of fear. So when a deaf teenage girl stumbled into a school begging for help after escaping a satanic cult, officials did all they could to protect her.

Monday 18th September 1989 started out like any ordinary day at the William B. Jack Elementary School in Portland, Maine. Lessons were being taught, the Monday blues had set in, and the weather was slowly turning to the Autumn chill.

But then something rather extraordinary happened. A teenage girl stumbled through the entrance of the school and was spotted by support teacher, Judi Fox. The girl, assumed to be between the ages of 14 to 16, was frightened, confused, and paranoid.

The girl stopped at the counter where Judi was working and signed something with her hands. Realising that she was signing for help, Judi called a teacher who could use sign language, to find out what was going on.

The teacher struggled to understand exactly what she was signing but worked out that the girl had escaped from someone. The teacher took her to a nearby school for deaf children, where the girl said her name was Toby Cole, and she had escaped a satanic cult who had kidnapped her three years earlier.

FBI involvement

Using a combination of drawings and sign language, she explained that she had been abducted from a foster home in California in 1986, and that the cult who took her travelled around the country, so she was unable to pinpoint exactly where she had been during those three years.

With satanic panic in full effect, the teachers had no reason not to believe her, so the local police became involved, and as it was a kidnapping case, the FBI were called in. FBI agent Paul Cavanagh took charge of the investigation and had close contact with Toby to establish what had happened.

Toby could not identify any of her kidnappers or members of the cult as she feared she may have been brainwashed after having been with them for so long. When Cavanagh went through some of her drawings, it became clear that the people she was with were involved in either satanic worship or some form of dark ritual abuse.

Except, Cavanagh had seen nothing like it before, and no cult he had come across with links to satanism were travelling the country constantly unseen. It seemed possible that Toby had escaped a group who were not already known to the FBI.

With the help of sign language experts, Toby claimed she was 15-years-old, and didn't know her birth name, as Toby Cole was the name given to her by her captors. This made things instantly difficult for police and Cavanagh, as there were no missing person's report for a Toby Cole anywhere in the country.

The FBI had no choice but to take her into protective custody and she was placed in a secure foster home by the Maine Human Services Department, until they could dive deeper into her past. Cavanagh quickly realised that evidence was thin on the ground, and that finding the girl's kidnappers might be too big of a task.

Bizarre revelation

He attempted to track Toby's movements in the days prior to appearing at the school, and why she had chosen the school to show up at. It could have meant that any vehicles belonging to her abductors were near the school, as she hadn't travelled too far to get there.

Cavanagh was concerned the culprits may have intended to recapture Toby and was worried the school could be a target. Toby believed she was born on Christmas Day 1974 but didn't know where in California she was born or where her parents were.

Many searches were carried out, and many investigatory teams in different parts of the country were utilised to trace any record of her, but there was no new information. As the days passed, and Toby couldn't offer any more details, the case went cold.

Then, less than a month later, Cavanagh and the police issued a statement to the press as they had made a bizarre discovery. 15-year-old Toby Cole was in fact a 27-year-old woman named Margaret Louise Herget.

Margaret had left her parents' home in Sandy, Oregon, in August, a month before she appeared at the school. When they were shown a newspaper image of Toby Cole, they immediately called the FBI to state that Toby was in fact their adult daughter.

Margaret had moved to Louisiana, but had no job set up, and no way of looking after herself. She was last seen in Metairie, Louisiana, just three days before appearing in Portland, Maine. But the strangeness didn't end there.

A broken mind

Margaret was confirmed to be hearing-impaired but not deaf so she was mostly able to understand what was going around her. She had also been previously diagnosed with various mental health disorders.

Toby Cole was one of many identities she had used in the past and would create lives and backgrounds for each one of them, though it remains unclear why she used various identities or what she intended to do with them. Her parents said she had long suffered from mental health issues.

However, despite having no money, and suffering from deteriorating mental health, Margaret managed to travel 1,620 miles (2,600km) from Metairie in Louisiana to Portland in Maine, before stumbling into the school.

There was simply no way she would have been able to travel there by herself, which led to further theories. Due to her mental health condition and ease at which she used multiple identities, it was possible she had hitchhiked to Maine in one vehicle or a succession of different vehicles.

Perhaps she was sexually assaulted during the journey or attacked in some other way, that led her to creating the story of Toby Cole and the satanic cult in her mind, to avoid facing the reality of what had happened. Perhaps the story was concocted with minimal effort, and that she needed help simply to return home.

For Cavanagh, it was one of the most unusual cases he worked on, despite no charges being brought against Margaret. There is the slim possibility that Margaret was indeed abducted and that she really did escape her captor to seek help at the school.

It seems an incredibly elaborate story for someone to have created in their mind. Perhaps the satanic element was influenced from stories in the press but then it remains unusual why she posed as a teenage girl. Not much is known about what happened to Margaret after the incident, but she was said to be living back home with her parents.

The tall tale of Toby Cole is on face value a simple hoax that ended up involving the FBI. But without Margaret ever explaining why she did it, there will always be a niggling sense that in the background, something horrific may have occurred.

FACTS!

Satanic panic was a term that began in the United States in the 1980s and had spread across the western world by the 1990s.

The term originated from a 1980 book called 'Michelle Remembers', in which satanic ritual abuse is revealed through hypnosis, but the book was later discredited as it had been mostly fictionalised.

The FBI employs over 35,000 people, and approximately 8,000 of those are Special Agents.

The Severed Feet of the Salish Sea

The unsettling discovery of severed feet and legs washing up along the Salish Sea led to rumours of serial killers and aliens, but the truth was even more disturbing.

The Salish Sea is known as a marginal sea, which is a body of water between ocean and land, similar to the English Channel. It is located in the Canadian Province of British Columbia and the U.S. state of Washington.

The sea covers an area of 18,000 square km (6,900 square miles) and averages out at 430ft deep (130m). It is a large, mostly unremarkable sea, were it not for the dozens of severed feet and legs that have washed ashore since 2007.

On 10th August 2007, a 12-year-old girl visiting the area with her family, found a blue and white running shoe on the shoreline of Jedediah Island. Inside the shoe was a sock and inside the sock was a severed foot.

Six days later, a holidaying couple walking on the shoreline of Gabriola Island found a black and white Reebok trainer. Inside was the severed foot of a man with size 12 feet. Police were stumped, as the two severed feet belonged to two different men.

The make of trainers were different and they contained two right feet. It was a considered a million-to-one chance that two severed feet would wash up along the islands and shorelines of the Salish Sea. Until more feet began to appear.

Feet feast

Six months later, in February 2008, another right foot was discovered inside a size 11 Nike trainer. Throughout 2008, another four severed feet washed up along the Salish Sea shorelines, leading locals to suspect an unusual serial killer was on the loose, one with a hatred of feet.

Along with the real feet, a number of pranks and hoaxes were carried out by locals, including putting dog bones into a shoe, stuffing it with seaweed and leaving it on the shoreline to confuse the police and media even more.

Up to January 2019, a total of 21 feet washed up on the shoreline of the Salish Sea, with four of them matching other feet found. This meant that the remains of 17 people had washed up on the shore, with no real explanation as to why – until the investigation dug deeper.

The investigation would soon discover the identity of many of the owners of the feet, but not all, which leads to some unusual theories we'll look at shortly. The first foot found by the 12-year-old girl belonged to a man who suffered from depression and so it was suspected he had taken his own life.

The fourth foot, found on 22nd May 2008, matched the one found in November of the same year. DNA profiling discovered they belonged to an unidentified woman who was suspected to have jumped from the Pattullo Bridge in New Westminster four years earlier.

The right foot found in February 2008 matched that of another foot found in June that year. DNA profiling again helped with the identification of a 21-year-old man who had been reported missing four years earlier. His feet had been mechanically severed at the ankle.

A foot found in Richmond on 27th October 2009 belonged to another man who was reported missing a year earlier. In August 2010, a child's foot with no shoe was found but DNA testing showed no match on the system. It was concluded the foot had been in the water for two months.

Enter the scientists

In November 2011, a group of campers found a severed leg in a freshwater pool at Sasamat Lake. An investigation discovered it belonged to a fisherman who had gone missing in 1987. A month later, a leg bone and foot were found in a plastic bag under the Ship Canal Bridge, but DNA profiling proved fruitless.

The last severed foot found in January 2019 belonged to a man who had been missing since 2016. Only some of the feet were linked to possible suicide cases but it didn't explain the others. Was there really a serial killer with a hatred of feet operating around the Salish Sea region?

Firstly, we have to look at how the feet may have got there, and it gets a little bit scientific. Bodies in water either float or sink, if they float then they are exposed to air and the bodies decompose differently to those that sink to the bottom of the ocean.

A study of the feet carried out by an investigator of the Coroners Service suggested that the bodies had sunk and decomposed under water. When the feet were naturally separated from the rest of the body, they rose due to the trainers or boots containing air pockets within their design.

A professor of oceanography developed a program that showed how an oil slick would spread throughout the Salish Sea. The test concluded that the area acts as a trap due to the tides and prevailing winds, which is why the feet made their way to the region.

Remaining unidentified

Of the 17 people whose feet have washed up on the shorelines of the Salish Sea, only seven have been identified as people who had gone missing in the years prior. Ten remain unidentified and murder has never been ruled out.

One theory pointed to the possibility of a container ship that had lost one of its containers as it passed near to the Salish Sea. The theory posits that the container held immigrants attempting to land in either the U.S. or Canada. However, no missing container has ever been reported, and the various types of feet and dates don't match up to the theory.

The most common theory in relation to the severed feet that haven't been identified was the 2004 Boxing Day Tsunami – which happened on the other side of the world. And yet, the theory holds some weight.

Some of the trainers with feet in them belonged to models that were manufactured and sold between 2003 and 2004. As almost 230,000 people died in the tragedy, it was deemed possible that various body parts could have travelled across the oceans, following the tides and winds and ending up at the Salish Sea.

Whatever the theories, ten victims remain unidentified to this day, whether by suicide, accident, or homicide. It remains entirely plausible that the feet belong to victims of crime, whose stories are yet to be told.

FACTS!

Canada's homicide rate fell to an all-time low in 2013 at 1.46 murders per 100,000 citizens but has since continued to rise dramatically, hitting 1.95 in 2020.

When a dead body ends up in water, the hands and feet easily detach from the arms and legs as the body decomposes, because the muscle attachments to the limbs are relatively weak.

Approximately 8.7million people live in the areas around the Salish Sea and it was first named as such by marine biologist Bert Webber in 1988.

Maniac Cop: The Murder of Missy Bevers

In one of modern times most eerie unsolved cold cases, a fitness instructor was killed in a local church by a person dressed in police SWAT gear.

Terri 'Missy' Bevers was no stranger to exercise, she had spent most of her adult life teaching others the benefits of a full body workout. Just before 4am on 18th April 2016, Missy left her home in Red Oak, Texas, and drove to the Creekside Church of Christ in Midlothian, 19 miles away.

She arrived at the church at 4.20am in the pouring rain and began setting up one of the rooms for her early morning Camp Gladiator class, which normally kicked off at 5am. Little did Missy know but someone else was already in the church waiting for her.

Just before 5am, the boot camp students began arriving. When they entered the room where the class was taking place, they found Missy lying on her back having been beaten and bludgeoned multiple times.

In a panic, the students called 911 and paramedics rushed to the church but it was too late as Missy was pronounced dead at the scene. When detectives arrived on scene, it was clear that Missy had been murdered, and the first suspicion was a robbery gone wrong.

When the church owners checked the building and its belongings, it appeared that nothing had been stolen, and Missy was still wearing her wedding ring. When investigators checked the CCTV from inside the church, they were shocked by what they saw.

Full tactical gear

Prior to retrieving the security footage, a search of the building revealed that many windows were broken and that the main door had been smashed through, meaning that Missy's murderer was already in the building when she arrived.

When police sat down to review the footage, the suspect was revealed. At 3.50am, footage showed a person wearing full police tactical or SWAT gear breaking into the church. The suspected burglar, who was masked in a full black helmet, began wandering the church.

The footage is eerie, as the person slowly and calmly wanders the dark hallways of the building, casually opening doors and occasionally smashing windows with the hammer they have in their hand. The person was estimated at being between 5'2" and 5'7" but the sex of the person could not be ascertained.

Whether the person inside the suit was male or female, they had an unusual gait which caused them to limp with their feet pointed slightly outwards. At 4.20am, Missy is seen entering the church and making her way to her classroom, unaware of the mysterious person traipsing through the building.

Within a few minutes of arriving in the darkened classroom, Missy was assaulted and beaten to death. Further CCTV footage showed a 2010-2012 Nissan Altima or Infiniti G37 stopping at a car park near to the church in the hours before the attack. The car didn't stay long but the owner has never been identified.

Witnesses saw a dark-coloured SUV driving from the church around 4.30am but the driver has also never been identified. Either one of the drivers of the vehicles could have been the killer. In the weeks that followed, police focused their attention on Missy's husband.

Suspects

Brandon Bevers had been having troubles in his marriage to Missy due to ongoing financial issues and cracks in their relationship. Police revealed they were talking to Brandon in relation to the case which caused the press and social media users to blame him.

But after a year-long investigation, police concluded that Brandon was not involved in his wife's death, and he was on a fishing trip in California at the time. Police stated that no member of her direct or indirect family were responsible, which began to raise questions. Most importantly, who had killed Missy?

Before they cleared the Bevers family of any wrongdoing, Brandon's father had taken a blood-soaked shirt to a dry cleaners in the days following the murder. He claimed he had broken up a dog fight, and the blood tests on the shirt confirmed he was telling the truth. There's not many killers dumb enough to take a bloody shirt to the dry cleaners, but police were looking everywhere.

Missy was active on the business social network LinkedIn, and when investigators went through her devices and accounts, they found she was talking to a man for three months before her murder, and that the messages were flirtatious in nature.

The man was interviewed and admitted to a friendship but was ruled out as a suspect due to his location and an alibi on the night of the murder. However, Missy had told friends in the days before her murder that she was receiving creepy and strange messages from a man she didn't know.

The final message was sent three days before the murder but police have never released the details of the message and it remains unclear if the sender was a suspect or just someone who was an annoyance to Missy.

Based on the SUV tip, investigators were led to former police officer Bobby Wayne Henry as a suspect as he owned a dark coloured SUV and still had his police tactical gear despite being fired in 2017 for sexual assault and possession of child pornography.

Despite the links, Bobby was several inches taller than the person in the CCTV footage which immediately ruled him out. Since 2017, the Missy murder case has fallen into the realm of the unsolved but it hasn't stopped investigators and web sleuths taking hold of the reigns.

Effective disguise

The tactical police gear disguise was so effective that no analysts could confirm without a shadow of a doubt if the person was male or female, though there were leaning more on the side of male due to the gait and the fact they killed with a hammer. Female killers rarely use objects that require strength, preferring methods such as poison.

Many still believe it was a robbery gone wrong but with no effort to take anything, the theory doesn't hold up. On the CCTV footage, the killer opens various doors without entering and passes by many others they don't bother to check, as if they are looking for something – or someone – specifically.

The casual walk of the person goes against every burglar/robber stereotype, who generally move quickly to get hold of their loot and get out before they're noticed, which makes the CCTV footage all that eerier. None of their actions make them out to be a burglar.

One theory points towards a teenage vandal as some of the inner windows were smashed but the person walks past many opportunities to vandalise and doesn't. And again, the casualness of the person's movements don't match someone who is intent on vandalising.

It most likely meant that Missy was the target of the killer and had been deliberately chosen by someone who knew she would be there alone. Due to her being known for fitness classes and her affinity for LinkedIn and Facebook, where she would share many details of her life, there is the possibility she may have had a stalker, which could have been the person who sent the creepy messages.

Maniac cop

Due to her fitness instructor career, she met many random members of the public which suggests she may have known her killer. The killer could have had their sexual advances rejected which led to them wanting to kill Missy so no one else could have her. But it remains only a theory.

It is unusual that the case has never been solved, due to its very clear security footage, witness statements regarding vehicles, and the names and locations of all Missy's students. But it is the SWAT gear that sets the murder aside from any other.

There would have been plenty of ways to disguise oneself when committing a crime and full police tactical gear is not the usual one. If the killer was attempting to confuse the investigation while hiding their identity, then it worked.

Some researchers have suggested the killer was a female due to the way they were holding the hammer on the footage. That the killer was overweight, as seen by the fit of the uniform and their gait, suggests that maybe they were someone who Missy had either embarrassed or ridiculed. Maybe they were waiting for Missy, to enact their revenge.

Who killed Missy and why remains a mystery to this day. It is unusual and creepy that there is so much evidence to go on and so little progress. The so-called maniac cop seems to have got away with murder, and if they are never caught in this life, then they will be judged in the next.

FACTS!

Camp Gladiator are a fitness movement dedicated to transforming lives through dynamic, fun, and challenging workouts. Trainers like Missy have to pass a specialised course in order to teach it.

To be eligible for SWAT, the recruit has to perform at a minimum, 12 pull-ups, 60 sit-ups in two minutes, 50 push-ups, run 2 miles in under 15 minutes and swim 200m in 7 minutes.

Missy's murder was the first in Midlothian, Texas, in seven years.

Murderous King of the Osage Hills

After the suspicious deaths of many Osage Indians, the FBI went undercover and unearthed a conspiracy involving multiple murder, insurance fraud, and a belief the Wild West was still alive.

Between 20 to 24 Osage Indians were killed during the early 1920s in a case so large that the FBI went undercover as cattlemen and salesman to blow open the case. They infiltrated the reservation and ended up solving the murders, but not before many more had been killed.

The Osage Nation, also known as the People of the Middle Waters, are a Midwestern Native American tribe of the Great Plains, who had been living in and around the Ohio and Mississippi river valleys since 700 BC.

From the 19th Century, the United States authorities forced most of the Indians to live in Osage County in Oklahoma. But the move had an unexpected outcome. As part of the agreement to move, the Osage became wealthy due to mineral rights on the land, which enraged local Americans.

On 27th May 1921, the decomposed body of 36-year-old Osage Native, Anna Brown, was found in a remote ravine in Northern Oklahoma, by two local hunters. She was the first known of the Osage Indian murders, but her death was put down as having died from alcohol poisoning.

Over time, Anna's death would prove instrumental in bringing down the empire of cattleman William Hale, who was accused by local criminal Kelsie Morrison. Morrison had killed Anna on the orders of Hale, who was seeking one thing and one thing only – the riches of the Osage Nation.

Taken out one by one

Despite Anna's death being put down as alcohol poisoning, a local undertaker discovered a bullet hole in the back of her head. A resulting investigation was played down by locals who were adamant she had died from natural causes and it went unsolved quickly.

As Anna had recently divorced her husband, the law at the time handed Anna's vast estate to her mother, Lizzie Q. Kyle. A week after Anna's body was found, the body of her cousin, Charles Whitehorn, was found nearby. He too had been shot dead.

And as if it wasn't obvious as to the motives of the murders, just two months after Anna's murder, her mother, Lizzie, was also killed under suspicious circumstances. But Lizzie's estate was much vaster that her daughter's.

Lizzie had inherited Anna's estate and the estate of her own late husband and his cousins. She was at one point, one of the richest people in all of Oklahoma. Hale, who was orchestrating the entire thing, was watching from a distance, as he methodically ordered the killings of more Osage Indians, as various estates passed down to them.

He was picking off the tribe in order to gain the riches for himself. In February 1923, Henry Roan, another of Anna's cousins, was shot dead as he sat in his car on the reservation. Roan was also known to have borrowed money from Hale, who made himself the beneficiary of Roan's estate. Which nowadays would have set off alarm bells with the local law enforcement.

In March of the same year, Anna's sister, her brother-in-law, and their servant, were killed by a large explosion that destroyed their Fairfax residence. One by one, the richest of the Osage Indians were being taken out.

Seeking help from the FBI

Hale had orchestrated his nephew, Ernest Burkhart, to marry one of Anna's sister's. Ernest had previously been Anna's boyfriend before she ditched him for another man. Hale realised that if a few more members of Anna's family died then the head rights of much of the land would fall to Ernest – and Hale.

From 1921 to 1923, another 13 suspicious deaths of Osage Indians occurred, all with tentative links to Hale but no one was able to prove it. Solving the cases proved difficult as Hale had planted false leads, threatened many of the locals, and paid others for their silence, which meant the locals would not talk to the FBI, then known as the Bureau of Investigation (BOI).

Some of the private detectives brought in by the Osage Tribal Council had been paid off by Hale or his associates to deliberately mislead the investigation. By 1924, more than sixty wealthy Osage Indians had died, from either natural causes or suspicious deaths.

As many had no heirs – because Hale was killing them off – the courts awarded the estates to their legal guardians. Which just so happened to be white lawyers and businessmen, who had involved themselves in the Indian's estates shortly before their deaths, with many appointed or coerced by Hale.

In 1924, the Osage elders sought assistance from the FBI due to the rising number of suspicious deaths among their people. An agent named Tom White became the public face of the investigation, while another four agents went undercover in one of the greatest undercover investigations in FBI history.

Infiltrators

The four agents worked undercover for two years. They consisted of a former New Mexico Sheriff, a former Texas Ranger, a lead detective, and a Ute Nation Indian who had previously been an undercover spy in the Mexican Revolution ten years earlier.

It was immediately clear that William Hale was linked to the murders but the FBI needed evidence in order to charge him. The undercover agents posed as an insurance salesman, a cattleman, oil prospector, and a herbal doctor, in order to get the evidence they needed.

The work they carried out while undercover, saw them gain the trust not only of the Osage Nation but the people who were actively seeking to usurp them. They learned that Hale was known as the King of the Osage Hills.

Hale had migrated from Texas to Osage County in the 1910s to find work in the oil fields, which had been discovered in the region in 1897. When they realised the Osage Indians were making a fortune from head rights – royalties paid by oil companies to use the land – Hale and his nephews saw money signs flash in front of their eyes.

They ended up infiltrating the Osage Nation to such a degree that they even began ordering the murders of white witnesses and people who knew about the plan. The undercover agents discovered a small criminal network of amateur contract killers and insurance fraudsters.

The Wild West of yesteryear

One of the agents worked his way into the company of Ernest Burkhart who confessed that Hale had killed some of the victims himself and ordered the killings of many others. Ernest also confessed to helping in some of the killings.

The agents managed to gather enough evidence to bring the case to the courts, and in 1926, William Hale, Ernest, contract killer John Ramsay, who shot dead Roan in his car, and Hale's other nephew, Bryan Burkhart, were arrested and charged with multiple murders.

Some of their acquaintances involved in the murders and insurance scams had either eloped by that point or had also died suspicious deaths, including Kelsie Morrison who had killed Anna. From 1926 to 1929, various court cases were in motion that caught the attention of the entire country.

Hale, Ernest, and Ramsay were convicted of multiple murders and sentenced to life imprisonment. Bryan, a lawyer, and another accomplice struck plea deals to provide evidence and walked free. Hale was paroled 18 years later in 1947 and died in Arizona in 1962, with none of the wealth he had accumulated.

Though the United States had moved away from the Frontier era of the Wild West, it appeared that Hale and his co-conspirators believed the Wild West was still with them. They were wrong. The head rights of the Osage Indians were managed by the federal government for the next eighty years.

In 2011, the Osage Nation won a settlement from the U.S. Government for $380million (USD) on the basis that federal management of the head rights had resulted in huge historical losses beginning with Hale's campaign of violence against them.

FACTS!

Today, there are approximately 24,000 Osage Indians, who mostly live in Oklahoma but many live and work in different American States.

The Osage Nation has an official website which can be found at https://www.osagenation-nsn.gov.

The first oil well in Oklahoma was called the 'Nellie Johnstone No.1' and began drawing oil on 15th April 1897. It was the first of thousands of oil wells in the state.

The Jammie Dodger Robbery

In a robbery worthy of bizarre true crime, a gang stole £20,000 worth of Jammie Dodgers, and when they were sentenced, shouted out 'anyone want a biscuit?'

Thtere are many robberies that make readers scratch their heads and wonder what the hell the robbers were thinking. But perhaps none more so than a five-strong gang who stole £20,000 ($25,000 USD) of sweet snacks from a Jammie Dodger factory.

In the United States, Jammie Dodgers are called Linzer cookies or Linzer torte, but the British being the British went with Jammie Dodger, though the biscuit originates from Austria. In the UK, they are produced by the Burton's Biscuits company, who are based in Cwmbran, South Wales.

The Burton food factory is a nondescript yellow building that is easily missed if you didn't know what you were looking for. But it had caught the attention of five robbers, and in June 2015, they put into action a robbery that would go down in history as one of the most unusual.

For reasons unknown, 35-year-old Anthony Edgerton called on four friends to help plan the robbery. Edgerton lived in Liverpool and recruited friend and former soldier, 28-year-old Kieron Price. To help them in the heist, they recruited Paul Price, 38, Stephen Burrow, 36, and Aaron Walsh, 25.

The five-strong mob spent a couple of weeks planning the robbery then drove from Liverpool to Cwmbran, almost 200 miles away. There, they carried out the audacious and yet bizarre plan to rob the Burton factory of thousands of pounds worth of snacks.

A simple plan

One month prior to the robbery, and in an effort to throw the resulting investigation off their trail, they stole a lorry and container from Kent, and a Network Rail Ford Transit van from the same area. The gang painted over the Network Rail signage and got to work planning the convoy. The lorry contained £43,000 worth of lager which the gang sold on the black market – and drank themselves.

The idea was to go in and swap the lorry out for another one that would be full of stock and simply drive off with it before transferring it to the Transit van. It was a daylight robbery that had no need for secrecy as they would be seen as making a legitimate pickup.

One of the gang pulled up at the security gate at 2.50am and feigned being confused as it was to be his first pickup. The security guard explained where he had to go and showed him which trailer was due for collection, unaware that a brazen theft was being put into action.

The gang member went to the distribution office of the factory and calmly stated that he had a collection for Liverpool. Somehow, he managed to convince the night shift worker that the collection was legitimate. At 3.10am, he drove back to the security gate with a new container attached to the back of the truck.

Not knowing any different, the security guard let him out. A few miles away on a remote layby, the rest of the gang were waiting with the transit van and another vehicle. They spent an hour transferring £20,000 ($25,000 USD) of sweet snacks and abandoning the Jammie Dodger trailer on the side of the road.

Anyone want a biscuit?

When the next shift arrived at the factory and looked at the collection orders for the night before, they were shocked to find that an unsanctioned pick up had been made. They called the police who arrived within minutes and got to work tracking the vehicles involved in the theft.

Throughout the course of the next few days, the investigatory team used traffic cameras and public CCTV to track the lorry and other vehicles all the way from Cwmbran to Liverpool. When they formed a suspect list, they used mobile cell towers to prove that each person had been involved in the theft.

All five men were arrested shortly after and charged with theft of goods and theft of vehicles. At their trial, the defence argued that two of the men were only peripherally involved and were not active in the actual robbery itself.

Kieron Price, who had been an active soldier with the Royal Engineers in Afghanistan was diagnosed with PTSD and was tempted into the plan as he knew how to drive heavy vehicles. He and Edgerton were also charged with the theft of the lorry in Kent.

Including the vehicle theft, the total value of goods stolen was in the region of £100,000 ($122,000). The gang were sentenced to a total of 11 years between them. Edgerton got 44 months, Paul got 40 months, Stephen and Aaron got 16, and Kieron got 18.

When they were led out of court, some members of the gang shouted out 'anyone want a biscuit?' Which concluded a bizarre low-value robbery that was referred to in the press as the Great Jammie Dodger Heist.

It was clear the gang were not going to get rich off the robbery and clearly didn't consult their fortune cookies. Though they had planned to sell the goods on, their plan crumbled just as quickly as a Jammie Dodger does in a cup of tea. Anyone for a biscuit?

FACTS!

Burton's Biscuits were founded in 1935 by Joseph Burton, helped by his grandfather who was operating a bakery in Leek, Staffordshire.

By 2020, the company employed over 2,000 people and hit sales of £275million. Aside from Jammie Dodgers, it was known for Maryland Cookies and Lyon & Thomas Fudge.

In 2021, Burton's Biscuits were purchased for £360million by the Ferrero company, who make Kinder Surprise, Nutella and Ferrero Rocher.

The Wartime Ripper

During wartime London, as the German bombs were raining down, a serial killer was at work who brought a new kind of darkness to the cold and lonely streets of the British Capital.

There is nothing worse than a city in fear of bombs falling from the sky, except perhaps a serial killer who took advantage of London's darkest hour to feed an evil desire for cold-blooded murder.

Known as the Blackout Killer or the Wartime Ripper, 27-year-old Gordon Cummins finally snapped and went on a killing spree across London that left six women dead and two severely injured, who barely managed to escape his clutches.

Coming just fifty years after the infamous Jack the Ripper murders, Cummins was seen as a new ripper, carving his way through the streets of London. Most of the murders took place in February 1942 but he was also suspected of killing two more a few months earlier in October 1941.

The air raids across Britain's major cities led to enforced blackout measures at night, blanketing the cities in darkness. It was under this cover of night that the Blackout Killer roamed the wartime streets seeking his innocent victims.

Extravagant persona

The blackouts had been imposed on various cities including London from September 1939 and were put in place to prevent enemy aircraft from being able to identify targets by sight. The blackouts remained in place until some restrictions were lifted in September 1944 as the German war machine weakened.

What set Cummins apart from the rest of his dark peers, was the brutality with which he carried out many of his murders. Some of the victims were so badly mutilated that police first thought they had been victims of a German bomb.

Born at the tail-end of the First World War, North Yorkshire-raised Cummins spent his childhood under the watchful eye of hard-working parents. His father ran a school for mentally challenged teenagers, and his mother was a housewife to four children.

Cummins had an unremarkable childhood but sought a career in chemistry before moving to Newcastle when he was 18 to take a job as an industrial chemist. Due to his poor time-keeping and anti-social behaviour, most-likely developed from his family's closeness to the delinquent school, he failed to keep down a job for more than a few months.

When he was 20, Cummins moved to London and took various jobs but found himself drawn into the large social life the city offered. His love for clubs, bars, and London women, led to him developing a persona for himself that lifted him from his working class roots to something he believed was more desirable.

He worked on a posh London accent and told wild stories of nights with multiple women and a fake heritage designed to show others how better he was than them. His extravagant persona was funded by petty theft, lifting him from his beer-swigging peers into a champagne lifestyle.

The Duke

At 21, Cummins joined the Royal Air Force and his posh persona led to many nicknames including The Duke and The Count. Though he annoyed most of his comrades with tales of grandeur, he trained hard enough to be selected for flight duty by the RAF selection board.

He also married Marjorie Stevens in 1936 but they never had children and their marriage was more out of convenience than love. She would continue to believe her husband was innocent of any crimes right up until her own death many years later.

Shortly before his arrest, Cummins was due to report for duty at an Air Crew Receiving Centre in Regent's Park, where he would have ultimately sat behind the controls of a Spitfire. But the Duke had gone down a path of murder and brutality that to this day raises the hairs on the back of the neck.

During the time of the first London murders in October 1941, Cummins was stationed in Colerne, Wiltshire, but whenever he went on leave, would head straight for central London to use prostitutes and revel in his own tales of magnificence and showmanship.

On the morning of 14th October 1941, following a bombing raid, workmen were searching through the rubble of a bombed house in Hampstead Road, close to Regents Park, when they stumbled upon a body. It was not unusual to find bodies in London during the war but there was something different about this one.

On top of some debris was the nude body of 19-year-old secretary Maple Churchward but she didn't show any signs of having been hurt during the bombing. Unsure of what they were looking at, the workmen called in the police, who confirmed that Maple had been strangled to death with her own knickers.

Despite being found nude, she had not been sexually assaulted. Police learned that Maple commonly slept with British servicemen, sometimes for money, other times for fun. She had last been seen at a bar in nearby Camden the previous evening.

Four days later, on the 17th, 48-year-old Edith Humphries was found by a friend lying in bed suffering from severe wounds. She had been stabbed in the head, hit with a heavy object multiple times, and her throat had been cut.

Edith was alive when she was rushed to hospital but died shortly after. There was no forced entry to her home and due to the closeness of both women's murders, police suspected the same killer had been responsible. Edith too was seen at a Central London bar the night before her murder.

The mutilator

Due to the severity of the war over London, the two murders were put on the backburner. During the following three months, Cummins was stationed at RAF St. John's Wood, commonly known as RAF Regents Park – a perfect location for him to escalate the murders.

On 8th February 1942, after a brief visit to his wife in nearby Southwark, Cummins headed out into war-torn London. A day later, another victim was found dead in an air-raid shelter. 41-year-old pharmacist Evelyn Hamilton was last seen drinking wine celebrating her 41st birthday at Marble Arch.

As she walked back to her boarding house, Cummins befriended and lured her to the air-raid shelter, where he became violent. He ripped off her clothes and manually strangled her to death. The autopsy showed that she tried to fight him off but was not sexually assaulted.

Her body was found by an electrician the following morning. Police discovered her handbag had been stolen, which may have contained upwards of £80, worth over £4,000 today. They learned that she was leaving London for Lincolnshire the next day and was winding up her personal affairs.

That same evening on 9th February, 34-year-old married nightclub hostess and prostitute Evelyn Oatley was approached by Cummins as she waited outside a restaurant in Shaftesbury. Just before midnight, the pair were seen entering an apartment building at 153 Wardour Street by another tenant.

The same tenant heard Oatley's radio turned up loud after midnight as Cummins was killing her and mutilating her body. He beat and strangled her into unconsciousness before cutting her throat from ear to ear. He then stripped her and laid her flat on the bed with her head hanging over the edge.

Then, with a razor blade, tin opener, and piece of a broken mirror, Cummins cut up her body, before raping her with an electric torch and curling tongs. Evidence found at the scene suggested he had used a total of seven blades to slice her body, which was found the next morning by electric meter workers.

The whistler

Already tainted by the horrors of war, police found fingerprints on the tin opener, mirror, and other items belonging to Oatley. But when they checked the fingerprints on the police database, there was no match, and for good reason – Cummins had never been arrested or convicted of a crime.

Which makes his sudden killing of many women that much stranger. On the next day, the 11th, 43-year-old prostitute Margaret Florence Lowe was murdered at her flat in Gosfield Street, Marylebone. She had last been seen by a neighbour in the early hours of the morning, accompanied by a client.

The same neighbour heard the client leave about an hour later, whistling away to himself, as if he'd had a night of fun. Lowe's body wouldn't be found until two days later when her 15-year-old daughter arrived home to find her on a bloody bed.

Her nude body had been positioned in such a way that she was on her back with her legs apart and knees bent upward. She had been brutally beaten to death and strangled with a silk stocking. And if police thought Oatley's murder was horrific, it was nothing compared to Lowe's.

Cummins had mutilated Lowe, partly when she was alive, but mostly after she had died. He used a razor blade, kitchen knife, dinner knife, and a fire poker, to stab and slice her body. All four weapons were left embedded in her body or nearby on the bed.

Her stomach had been sliced open with such severity that her organs were exposed, along with multiple lacerations and cuts to her groin. A large wax candle had also been inserted into her. That the suspect walked away from the scene whistling happily sent chills down the investigators spines.

Unstoppable

Fingerprints were lifted and matched those from the Oatley crime scene. Autopsies confirmed the suspect was left-handed, which Cummins was, but he was able to hide himself away in the arms of RAF Regent's Park.

One day after Lowe's horrific death, on 12th February, 25-year-old prostitute Catherine Mulcahy was attacked by Cummins in her own home, after he had paid for her services. As Mulcahy stripped, Cummins attacked her and pushed her to the bed attempting to strangle her.

But Mulcahy was strong enough to fight him off and ran screaming from the flat. She later claimed that Cummins's eyes had changed from a well-to-do gentleman to a monster within seconds. Cummins exited the flat and tried to give her more money then fled before police arrived.

It was perhaps a fortunate case of luck that Cummins had forgotten to put back on his RAF belt, which was found in Mulcahy's apartment. The same evening, Cummins hooked up with 32-year-old prostitute Doris Jouannet, who took him back to her flat in Bayswater. She had referred to Cummins as a client she called 'The Captain'.

The following day, Jouannet's husband with the help of a friend who was a police officer, broke down her bedroom door and discovered her nude body on the bed she used to entertain clients. The same brutality had been inflicted on Jouannet,

She had been strangled with a silk stocking, her jaw had been broken off due to the savagery of the attack, and her body had been mutilated with various sharp instruments, including a razor blade and multiple knives. Some of the flesh underneath her breasts had been carved off.

Once again, fingerprints taken from the scene matched those of the other murders. But police were already closing in due to Cummins having left the RAF belt at Mulcahy's flat.

Prelude to an end

The press initially gave little service to the story of the murderer, but with the killings so close together, Cummins was referred to as the Blackout Killer, and the following day made headlines across the entire country.

Even with police investigating him, and the press writing about the murders, for some reason known only to Cummins, he just couldn't stop killing, and less than a day after Jouannet's murder, he attacked another woman.

On the 13th, Cummins lured Margaret Heywood to join him for a drink in a bar in Piccadilly. When they left the bar, he attempted to forcibly direct Heywood to a nearby air raid shelter but she tried to fight him off. Cummins then pushed her into a doorway and strangled her into unconsciousness.

The attack was stopped when a passing beer bottle deliveryman spotted Cummins rifling through Heywood's handbag. The deliveryman came to the rescue forcing Cummins to flee, and in doing so he left behind his RAF gas mask and rucksack in the doorway. To cover himself later, Cummins stole another serviceman's gas mask and rucksack.

Fortunately, Heywood survived the attack and would later be able to identify Cummins. When police got hold of the gas mask and rucksack, they contacted the local RAF bases who ultimately led them to Cummins, due to the issue numbers on the military gear.

On Valentine's morning, Cummins was arrested but concocted a fake story that he was out drinking whisky with another serviceman whose name he coincidentally couldn't recall. He claimed to have no memory of attacking Heywood but wished to apologise to her if he had done.

While he was under arrest for committing grievous bodily harm, detectives realised they could have the Blackout Killer in custody, so they jumped into full-on investigatory mode to prove it.

Irrefutable evidence

The RAF Regent's Park passbook was signed by Cummins on all the nights that the murders and attacks happened, but fellow servicemen claimed they all had each other's backs and falsified documents with pencil should any one of them return after a military-enforced curfew.

Police later discovered that Cummins and other servicemen would sneak out of the base at night and not return until the early hours. When police searched his belongings they found most of the proof they were looking for.

Cummings had been taking souvenirs from each of his victims including a metal cigarette case belonging to

Oatley along with a picture of her mother. There were traces of blood on one of his unwashed shirts, and his military uniform had traces of brick dust only found in the air raid shelter were Hamilton's body was found.

But more importantly, all the fingerprints belonging to the suspect in the four February murders were a match with Cummins. They also discovered that new £1 notes had been given to Mulcahy by her attacker. Investigators tracked the serial numbers and discovered the notes were brand new and had been issued via the RAF base to Cummins.

Heywood identified Cummins in a line-up and the police had everything they needed to lay multiple counts of murder at his feet. In front of them was not only one of the most brutal killers of 1940s London but a terrifying serial killer who offered no real motive for his crimes beyond circumstance.

Serial killer

Cummins still maintained his innocence when he was charged with murder on the 16th of February and put together various stories to lay the blame at the feet of other servicemen who had 'clearly' swapped RAF-issued clothing and accessories with him to pin the blame on him.

In April 1942, Cummins went on trial for the murder of Oatley and pleaded not guilty. With all the witnesses, autopsies, and forensic evidence, there was no way Cummins was going to get away with it.

He was found guilty of the murder of Oatley, and in the interests of the British public, was sentenced to death.

On 25th June 1942, Cummins was led to the gallows at Wandsworth prison where he was hanged. He maintained his innocence right up until the end.

He was eventually linked with the other murders, the two in October 1941 and three in February 1942. That he was already sentenced to death meant that any other convictions would not have changed the ultimate outcome.

He remains one of Britain's most curious and brutal serial killer's, having claimed one more victim than Jack the Ripper, bringing darkness to a city where there were already horrors at every turn.

FACTS!

Cummins was the only convicted murderer to be executed during an air raid.

Wandsworth prison was the site of 135 executions from 1878 to 1961.

It was believed that Cummins used the sound of German air raid sirens to claim his victims when they were at their weakest.

The Pendle Witches

In the summer of 1612, ten witches, six from two rival families, were found guilty of murder and witchcraft and executed at Gallows Hill, in one of the best-recorded witch trials in history.

Lancaster has a long and dark history and wasn't granted city status until 1937, its castle was still being used as a prison as recently as 2011. The city had a grim reputation for carrying out executions and is second only to London for the most people executed in England, giving it the unfortunate moniker of 'the hanging town'.

Perhaps the best known of the witch trials was the 17th Century trials of the Pendle witches, because in a rare move at the time, the entire trial and case were documented in a book titled, '*The Wonderfull Discoverie of Witches in the Countie of Lancaster.*' The spelling is as it was back then.

It was written by the clerk of the court, Thomas Potts, and due to its detailed account of the trials, the legend of the Pendle witches is not so much legend, but fact, at least, in relation to the trial itself. The notion that the 10 people executed from the trials were real witches depends very much where one stands on the spectrum of the occult or paranormal.

Bear in mind that in the 17th Century, the humble hedgehog was associated with witchcraft, with some people believing that a hedgehog was a witch in disguise and could shape-shift and venture into any building to cause harm to others. Though it should be noted that witches were associated with many small animals – demons sent out to do their bidding.

In 1612, the Pendle witch trials took place, in which 12 people were accused of witchcraft, who lived in and around the Pendle Hill region of Lancashire. In total, they were charged with the murders of ten people using the dark magic of witchcraft. One died in prison while awaiting trial, and of the 11 remaining witches, only one was found not guilty. The other 10 were executed by hanging.

Rival families

Six of the 11 witches on trial came from two rival families, the Demdike's and the Chattox's, who were overseen by two elderly widows. Elizabeth Southerns was known as Old Demdike and had been known as a witch for over 50 years, which makes it surprising that she wasn't executed sooner.

However, in the 16th to 17th Centuries in England, it was a mostly accepted part of village life that there was a healer in the village who practiced unorthodox magic and sold herbs and medicines. Witchcraft was made a capital offence in Britain in 1563, but Pope Innocent VIII had deemed it heresy since 1484.

From 1484 to the 1750's, over 200,000 witches were tortured, burned alive, or executed in Western Europe. It might be surprising to learn that only 500 of those took place in England, 1,500 in Scotland, and only five in Wales.

Old Demdike's rival was Anne Whittle, known as Mother Chattox, and they fought with each other over business in the village, as both families were offering similar services. In fact, many of the accusations of witchcraft came from members of both families, as they sought to stop the competition, so, in some way, the trials were caused by themselves.

The event that led to the Pendle witch trials took place on 21st March 1612, when Old Demdike's granddaughter, Alizon Device, was out walking in Trawden Forest. She approached a street seller named John Law, and asked him for some pins, which were sometimes used in witchcraft to treat a variety of ailments.

Law refused to sell her the pins and carried on his way but a few moments later, he collapsed. Alizon watched as he managed to get back to his feet and stumble into a local Inn. She believed she had caused the man to fall down with her powers and thought she was more powerful than she first realised. Though, in reality, John Law may have suffered a mild stroke.

Bickering of witches

John's son accosted Alizon a couple of days later and took her to see his father. While there, believing she had used her powers to make him fall down, she confessed to hurting him using witchcraft and begged for forgiveness. As word got around that Old Demdike's granddaughter had used witchcraft on another person, the story caught the attention of Roger Nowell, who was the justice of the peace for Pendle – a judicial officer of a lower court.

Alizon, her brother James, and their mother Elizabeth Device were summoned by Nowell to appear in court on 30th March. There, Alizon confessed she had sold her soul to the Devil and used her connection with the dark lord to make John Law fall to the ground. Elizabeth confessed that her mother, Old Demdike, had a mark on her body that was left by the Devil sucking her blood.

Alizon quickly realised that instead of giving up her entire family, she could also get the Chattox family charged with witchcraft – and an opportunity for revenge. In the ten years prior to the John Law incident, members of the Chattox family had stolen goods from Device's home and caused damage to their property. Alizon also accused the family of killing five men, including her own father who died in 1601.

She claimed that her father was so scared of Mother Chattox that he agreed to give her a bag of oatmeal each year in return for leaving his family alone. In 1601, he forgot to hand over the oatmeal and became ill. On his deathbed, he blamed Mother Chattox for his illness, which eventually killed him.

On 2nd April 1612, Old Demdike and Mother Chattox were taken from their home and appeared in court, along with Chattox's daughter, Anne Redferne. Both matriarchs were blind and in their eighties, a noble age in the 17th Century. Both women confessed to selling their souls to the devil but that the other was responsible for deaths in the region.

The following day, after hearing all the evidence and statements, Nowell and the judge detained Alizon, Anne, Old Demdike and Mother Chattox and set a date for trial. While awaiting trial, Old Demdike died in the dungeons of Lancaster Castle, unable to live with the dark, damp conditions.

My mother is a witch

Before the trial, James Device, Alizon's brother, stole a neighbours sheep which caused Nowell to investigate the family further. Eight more people were committed to the same trial, including Elizabeth Device, James Device, Alice Nutter, Katherine Hewitt,

Jane Bulcock and her son John, Alice Grey and Jennet Preston, who had all met at Malkin Tower to allegedly plan various murders. Preston was sent to trial in York as she lived in Yorkshire, and the other seven were sent to Lancaster prison to join the other three.

Preston's trial took place first in York on 27th July 1612. It materialised that she had met James Device to plan the murder of a Thomas Lister, a local landowner close to York, who Preston had fought with for years. When she was taken to see Lister's body, it was said that the corpse bled fresh blood from its orifices. Preston was executed two days later by hanging, the first of ten executions.

The pendle witch trials took place between 17th and 19th August 1612, and ultimately rested on the evidence given by nine-year-old Jennet Device, who was allowed to testify as witch trials fell under different rules than other trials. She identified all the people who had attended the murder meeting at Malkin Tower and gave evidence against her own mother, Elizabeth.

'My mother is a witch and that I know to be true. I have seen her spirit in the likeness of a brown dog, which she calls Ball. The dog did ask what she would have him do, and she answered that she would have him help her to kill.' – Jennet Device

When Elizabeth heard her daughter testify against her, she had to be physically removed from the court as she was screaming and cursing at her daughter with a maniacal look on her face. Modern investigators posit that Jennet was coerced to testify but it has never been proven.

City of witches

Alice Grey was the only person in the trial who was found not guilty. She was accused alongside Katherine Hewitt of murdering Anne Foulds the year before. Alice was said to have been at the meeting at Malkin Tower but was not deemed to be involved in any witchcraft and was ultimately acquitted. Katherine was found guilty and sentenced to death and was linked with a child murder a few years earlier.

Mother Chattox was found guilty of the murder of Robert Nutter, after a former house guest, James Robinson, accused Chattox of turning his beer sour and witnessed her take part in dark magic. Upon his testimony, Anne broke down and confessed she had sold her soul to the Devil.

James Device was found guilty of the murders of villagers Anne Townley and John Duckworth, after his nine-year-old sister Jennet confessed she had seen James talking with a black dog to help him conjure up a spell to kill Townley.

Anne Redferne was found guilty of the murder of Robert Nutter's father, Christopher, after various witnesses came forward to claim that Anne was a far more dangerous witch than her mother, Old Demdike.

Jane Bulcock and her son were found guilty of witchcraft and the murder of Jennet Deane purely on the basis of testimony from Jennet Device, who identified them as being at the meeting. Alice Nutter was found guilty of the murder of Henry Mitton, despite not confessing or having no evidence against her aside from Jennet Device's identification of her.

When John Law was brought in as a witness in the case of Alizon Device, Alizon saw him and immediately fell to her knees to beg for forgiveness, confessing her sins upon the world. She was the only person on trial who truly believed she had the power of a witch.

On 20th August 1612, Alizon, Elizabeth, and James Device, Anne Redferne, Alice Nutter, Katherine Hewitt, John and Jane Bulcock, and Mother Chattox were led to an open field and hanged at Gallows Hill in Lancaster.

The Pendle witch trials are one of the most recorded witch trials in history and shows just how far the establishment went to rid witches from the land. It's an unusual story, in that most of the accusations and evidence came from members of the same family, rival families, and friends. If they hadn't accused each other of witchcraft then the trials may not have ever taken place.

FACTS!

In Lancaster today, over 400 years later, the Pendle witches remain a big draw to the city and are responsible for increased tourism to the area.

The city is home to the Pendle Witch Trail which leads to Lancaster Castle, a local bus called The Witch Way, and a beer called the Pendle Witches Brew.

An annual Halloween gathering takes place on Gallows Hill, where the witches were executed.

Burning of Mary Channing

A young woman obsessed with free money, parties, and multiple lovers, poisoned her husband and was burned at the stake for her troubles in front of thousands of people.

Born in 1687 to hard working and wealthy parents in Dorchester, England, Mary Brookes (later Channing) was provided with a healthy and happy childhood. Though Dorchester would evolve to become the jewel in the crown of the county of Dorset, it was already marred by darkness.

Just two years before Mary's birth, 312 prisoners of the Monmouth Rebellion were tried in the town, leading to 74 men being hung in public. It was an age of war and violence under the ever-persisting threat of witchcraft.

Despite her somewhat wealthy childhood, Mary had a most unremarkable upbringing, with one of the highlights being that she was taught to read and write, a rarity in Dorchester for a young girl at the time.

But when she reached her teenage years, Mary was already unkempt, untidy in appearance and known to be sexually active. Her parents constantly opened new businesses to keep the family going and avoid the pitfalls of 17th Century working class Britons, leaving Mary mostly on her own.

Husband to control her

It was this lack of parental direction that many blamed for Mary's later actions, enabled by parents who believed in materialism over spiritualism. With their new wealth, they sent her on visits to London to broaden her view of the world and experience what could be possible for her future.

After many trips around the country, she settled back in Dorchester and spent her time in the company of women and men who were free and spirited like her, much to her parent's distaste. She fell for one of her young neighbours and gave him lavish gifts to win his affection.

Their sexual encounters were so passionate that the man's own neighbours complained of the noise they would make. When Mary's parents received word of her unruly behaviour, they made the decision to marry her off – but not to the neighbour.

Her parents chose a grocer named Thomas Channing, as they knew the family. They believed that a husband like Thomas would be able to control her and give her a better standing in the town beyond the mischief and anti-social behaviour she was beginning to elicit.

On 15th January 1704, 17-year-old Mary reluctantly married Thomas at a downbeat wedding ceremony. Thomas had tried to change her ways but failed from the outset. Within a month of being married, Mary was carrying on her love affair with the young neighbour.

Lewd and indecent

As her hatred of her parents grew, and needing money to continue her illicit affair, she tried to convince some of her friends to help rob her own parents. They didn't agree and word spread further around town that Mary was leading a life of crime and was bringing the name of Dorchester into disrepute.

To facilitate her affair, she paid off local homeowners so she could use their homes for meetings with her lover. As her passion for adulterous relationships grew, she found comfort in the arms of many different men and gained access to their homes, lives, and friends.

Soon, Mary was known around town as the source of parties and reckless abandon. As such, homeowners were more willing to rent out their homes in order to lay on lavish parties that involved dancing, alcohol, and sex.

By this point, the Channing family had become aware of Mary's lifestyle and privately turned against her but stood by Thomas in the hope that he might receive financial favour from Mary's family. Mary's father then said he would bestow nothing on them but his blessing.

As a humbled wife, Mary had to travel around the country accompanying Thomas in his business meetings and work. But whenever she got the opportunity, she returned back to Dorchester and into the arms of her many lovers, returning to her pre-marriage ways.

It was written in a story about Mary after her execution that at many private engagements, her conversation was so lewd and her actions so indecent that even the men who were present were embarrassed and ashamed to be in her company.

The poisoning

When Thomas's father cut off a line of credit to Thomas and Mary, it set in motion a plan of murder. Unable to afford her lavish lifestyle without the financial assistance from her husband and his family, Mary decided to kill her husband and claim his inheritance and wealth for herself.

On Monday 16th April 1705, Mary purchased some mercury from an apothecary's assistant, when she was told there was no rat poison available. The next morning, as Thomas sat down for breakfast, Mary served him a dish of rice milk laced with a substantial part of the mercury, a toxic metal that is poisonous when consumed in large quantities.

Just a couple of spoonful's was all it took to make Thomas ill, due to the amount of poison that Mary had put into the milk. She washed everything up and wiped down any trace of evidence as Thomas became violently ill, vomiting in the front garden of their home.

Bizarrely, a neighbour's dog thought the vomit was food and ate some of it. When the dog became ill as well, the neighbours suspected foul play was afoot. Though terribly ill, Thomas remained alive but bedridden.

As the days passed, and Mary fed him more of the poison, Thomas concluded that his own wife was indeed poisoning him. He wrote a will leaving his entire estate to his father, and just one shilling to Mary, a token amount to acknowledge that she was not to receive a shilling more.

By the Saturday, Thomas had succumbed to the pain of the poison and passed away having suffered terribly. His father was already suspicious and ordered an autopsy to ascertain the true cause of death. When it turned out that Thomas had poison coursing through his veins, there was only one suspect.

Search party

The local police searched Dorchester for Mary but initially couldn't find her. Realising she had been rumbled, Mary eloped four miles to the next parish where she spent most of the day in a wooded area hiding among the trees.

Thomas's father raised a search party to rampage through Dorchester and the surrounding areas to find the witch that had killed his son. They searched the woods where she had been seen but Mary had secretly, and under cover of night, returned to Dorchester.

When she was captured, she claimed she never realised her husband had died and was innocent of any accusations laid at her feet. She was charged with Thomas's murder and held in the local jail as investigators tried to work out the truth of what had happened.

One of Mary's brothers lied to police and said that Thomas had asked him to get the poison so he could use it for his business. The story was almost believed except at that exact time, the apothecary assistant had come forward and stated that Mary had purchased mercury.

The trial began on 28th July 1705 in Dorchester where Mary pleaded not guilty to the murder of her husband. Many witnesses were called forward to testify against Mary's character and her unwanted relationship with her husband. The fact that Thomas had changed the will shortly before his death meant he became a posthumous witness in his own murder.

Mary was seen preparing all of Thomas's meals before his death. She was also seen hiding from the search party that went out to look for her. It was expected she would be found guilty but the sentence was somewhat unexpected.

Maumbury Rings

Her lover also gave evidence that he was with her on many nights while she was married and that she spoke of her husband with disdain. She had also gifted her lover and others in the town expensive goods, paid for by her husband's finances, yet she would not bestow her husband with such gifts.

The nail in the coffin was the testimony of the apothecary assistant who confirmed that Mary was looking for rat poison but purchased mercury – the poison found in Thomas's blood. Unusually for the time period, Mary acted as her own defence and questioned the witnesses herself, which didn't help as she was found guilty.

She was sentenced to death, to be burned alive at the stake. However, unknown to the court, Mary was pregnant with the child of an unidentified father. Her sentence was postponed until after she gave birth. When her son arrived, her family begged the courts for leniency and asked for a pardon which was never given despite an appeal.

During the appeal, she managed to get herself baptised by a local clergyman, who also begged the courts to change the sentence. The clergyman wrote to the Bishop of Bristol but no further intervention was to come.

On 21st March 1706, Mary Channing was led to the neolithic henge site of Maumbury Rings in the town to be executed. Two men had already been executed in the hour before her, one for stealing and another for murder.

A crowd of thousands had gathered for Mary's execution, with some reports stating as many as

10,000, though exact numbers have never been agreed. When pressed for a confession, she continued to maintain her innocence.

At five in the afternoon, Mary was fixed to the stake and manually strangled to death – a small mercy requested by the church. When she was found to be dead, the firewood was kindled and the crowds watched her burn to ash.

FACTS!

Dorchester's roots go back to prehistoric times with different tribes making it their settlement since 4000 BC. The Durotriges tribe were living there when the Romans arrived in 43 AD.

The population of Dorchester in 2021 was 21,580 and was made up of 95% white British.

The Monmouth Rebellion was an attempt to overthrow James II from May to July 1685. Over 1,500 people were killed.

Codename Piccadilly and the Umbrella Murder

While waiting for a bus in London, a Bulgarian writer and journalist was assassinated after being stabbed in the thigh with the poisonous tip of an umbrella, by an assassin codenamed Piccadilly.

I n what became known as the Umbrella Murder, 49-year-old Georgi Ivanov Markov was murdered by an unidentified assassin, who used a poisoned pellet hidden in the tip of an umbrella, on Waterloo Bridge, London, in 1978.

Born in 1929, in the Sofia neighbourhood of Knyazhevo in Bulgaria, Markov went on to become a chemical engineer and a technical schoolteacher. After fallen ill with tuberculosis at the age of 19, he was forced to leave his academic career, upon which he turned to writing.

He published his first novel in 1957 and within a few years, was well-known in Bulgaria due to the many awards he was accumulating for his work. He caught the attention of Bulgarian officials when one of his books was halted mid-publication due to being anti-Lenin, and some of his books were subsequently banned for showing dissent against communism.

Due to his popularity, Markov was one of the authors approached by Bulgarian leader Todor Zhivkov to fill his books with propaganda for the Bulgarian regime. Unlike other authors who were approached, Markov declined, which put him on the Bulgarian watchlist.

Realising he had fallen out with the Bulgarian regime, Markov left the country in 1969 and moved to Italy where his brother lived, intending to return to Bulgaria when the heat on him had died down.

In 1971, Bulgarian authorities refused to renew his passport and Markov found himself without a nation. In September of that year, he moved to London, where he would meet his fate.

Listless flock of sheep

Markov picked up the English language quickly and soon found himself working as a journalist for the Bulgarian wing of the BBC World Service. Due to his move to London, in 1972, Markov was suspended from the Union of Bulgarian Writers.

Bulgarian officials had forced the suspension as Markov was seen as a traitor for moving to the West, despite Bulgaria not renewing his passport. Following on from the suspension, Markov was sentenced to six-and-a-half-years in prison for defection but was tried 'in absentia', meaning he didn't need to be present for the conviction.

After taking time off from the BBC to marry Annabel Dike in 1975 and having one daughter with her, Markov began spreading anti-Bulgarian rhetoric. But he didn't take the campaign against him lying down, in fact, he decided to write and talk about it.

Between 1975 and 1978, Markov penned a series of essays, reports and books about life in communist Bulgaria, including criticisms of the government and their leader Todor Zhivkov. For three years, he continued his criticism of Bulgaria, which in turn, made him an enemy of the state.

'We have seen how personality vanishes, how individuality is destroyed, how the spiritual life of a whole people is corrupted to turn them into a listless flock of sheep.' – Markov.

Despite his very public outrage at the Bulgarian authorities, Markov would confide in friends and colleagues at the BBC that he was in fear of his life and that his words would one day make him a target for assassination. A fear that would soon prove to be true.

Assassination

On 7th September 1978, Markov walked along Waterloo Bridge in London and waited at a bus stop to travel to his job at the BBC. While waiting for the bus, he felt a quick sharp pain on the back of his thigh and turned to see a man holding an umbrella walking away from him.

He watched the man hurriedly cross the road and climb into a taxi but didn't think anymore of the unusual incident until later that day. Initially, Markov had put it down to a clumsy man who hadn't realised what he had done.

A few hours later, while at work at the BBC World Service offices, he realised the pain hadn't gone down and a small red bump had begun to form on the back of his thigh. He took one of his friends and colleagues, Teo Lirkoff, to one side, to tell him what had happened and how unusual it was.

He said that a well-built man with a foreign accent had pushed him in the leg with the point of his umbrella and Markov heard the man say that he was sorry before he walked off. When the workday ended, Markov was in pain and began to feel weak.

Markov barely managed it back to his home in South London where his wife put him to bed. In the middle of the night, he developed a high fever, and due to his deteriorating condition, was admitted to St. James Hospital in Balham.

His symptoms were said to be similar to a bite from a venomous snake but doctors couldn't uncover the cause of the illness. Despite doctors attempting to save his life, Markov died of a massive heart attack four days later on 11th September. It was then that the investigation began.

Death by ricin

The police ordered an autopsy due to the story that Markov had told friends and family. A previous x-ray of Markov's leg had not shown anything untoward. During the autopsy, a tissue sample was taken from the red area on Markov's leg, along with another tissue from the other leg at the same area.

Still, there was nothing unusual showing up, so the samples were sent to the Porton Down chemical and biological weapons laboratory in Wiltshire. One of the medical officers at the facility found a tiny pellet in the tissue sample, which measured less than two millimetres in diameter.

The design of the pellet was seen by some medical officers as flawless. It was composed of 90% platinum and 10% iridium and had two holes drilled through it making an X-like inner hole. The hole would have been filled with poison and covered up with a sugary substance that would have melted once inside Markov's flesh, exposing the poison to his system. The likely poison; ricin.

Ricin is a toxic protein found in the seeds of the castor-oil plant and remains one of the most toxic substances known to man. If one was to chew and ingest castor beans or seeds then they would die within 36 to 72 hours.

The road to death by ricin is not pretty. First come the hallucinations, followed by tightness in the chest, coughing, nausea, severe dehydration, then liver and renal failure. The lungs begin to fail and the body's red cells are destroyed, before succumbing to either respiratory or heart failure.

Astonishingly, there is no antidote for ricin poisoning and any treatment given to a sufferer is to make their last few hours as comfortable as possible. But Markov wasn't the first to be injected with a ricin-filled pellet.

Previous attack

Ten days before Markov's murder, former head of the Paris Bureau of the Bulgarian State Radio and TV network, Vladimir Kostov, was attacked in a similar fashion, as he was leaving the Arc de Triomphe Metro station in Paris.

On August 27th, Kostov heard a crack that sounded like an airgun and felt a sharp pain on the right side of his back. The wound became inflamed but he recovered in hospital and survived. Kostov was also a Bulgarian defector.

In Kostov's case, the pellet had been removed from his back but any poisonous material inside the pellet did not spread as the sugary substance covering the holes didn't melt. The two pellets were later examined in London and it was discovered they were exactly the same size and had the same details, meaning the same assassin was likely to be responsible.

The umbrella murder made headlines all over the world, due to its James Bond style operation, and that the death had come towards the end of the Cold War. The story remained in the headlines for months, forcing a public enquiry into what had happened.

The nature of the assassination meant that Soviet KGB or Bulgarian secret services were suspected of being involved in the attack, which meant that a foreign state had committed murder on British soil, causing controversy across the board.

In early 1979, the enquiry concluded that Markov had died a slow and painful death as a result of a rare poison seeping into his bloodstream. But the enquiry did not conclude with a verdict of murder or manslaughter as it was deemed possible that Markov could have poisoned himself.

Codename Piccadilly

The conclusion of the enquiry again made international headlines as no one else believed that Markov had killed himself in such a fashion, and over time, they were proved right. Many years later, a KGB defector named Oleg Kalugin claimed that the KGB had arranged the murder and had been given options including a jelly to rub on Markov's skin.

Kalugin went onto confirm that Markov had been killed with an umbrella gun. 15 years later, the Times newspaper published an article in which they believed the assassin was an Italian named Francesco Gullino, a known smuggler given the choice of going to a Bulgarian prison or becoming a secret agent in the West, specifically Britain.

In 1993, Gullino was arrested by British and Danish police in Copenhagen and admitted to being in London when Markov was murdered but denied any involvement. Shortly after his release. Gullino eloped and remained off the grid – until August 2021 when he was found dead in an apartment in Austria.

In 2008, due to public interest, British police reopened the Markov file and travelled to Bulgaria, which had ended its communist rule way back in 1990. Investigators managed to speak to various individuals and uncovered secret police files from the time that identified Markov's killer as an agent code-named 'Piccadilly'. To this day, the identity of 'Piccadilly' remains a mystery.

FACTS!

There is an exhibit on display at the International Spy Museum in Washington that shows an umbrella gun similar to the one used to kill Markov.

In 2021, the City of London had a crime rate of 665 crimes per 1,000 people and remains one of the country's most dangerous areas for violent crime.

For London as a whole, the crime rate for 2021 was 87 per 1,000 residents, slightly higher than the national average of 77 per 1,000.

The Monster Butler & The Sidekick

Scottish serial killer Archibald Hall, known as The Monster Butler, killed five people in the late 1970s while working for the British upper class, with help from his sidekick, Kitto.

Archibald Thomson Hall was known as The Monster Butler, who committed his crimes whilst working for the British upper class and killed five people to protect his identity in order to continue his life of luxury.

Born in Glasgow, Scotland, in 1924, Hall began his criminal career at an early age and moved from thieving from local shops to breaking and entering homes in the middle of the night. In his formative years he realised he was bisexual and moved to London where he became well known in the underground gay scene of the 1950s to 1970s.

He was convicted of a jewellery theft in the 1960s and sent to prison for ten years before escaping five years later. He was recaptured and served out his sentence. While there, he studied antiques and learned the etiquette of the aristocracy and upper classes so that he could hide his identity once he was released.

He also took elocution lessons to soften his Scottish accent. He was in and out of prison for various crimes including robbery. In 1975, following on from his most recent release, he moved back to Scotland and used the name Roy Fontaine, named after his favourite actress Joan Fontaine.

Hall was employed as a butler to Margaret Hudson who was the widow of conservative politician Austin Hudson. Margaret lived at the lavish Kirtleton House in Dumfriesshire and Hall was more than happy to work there. He had initially planned to steal the most valuable items in the house and elope.

However, he changed his mind when he realised he really enjoyed working for Margaret and fell in love with being a butler. Then, in 1977, one of Hall's former cellmates, David Wright, was employed as a groundskeeper, which panicked Hall, as Wright knew his true identity.

Killing to hide his identity

While robbing some jewellery, Wright threatened to tell the lady of the house about Hall's previous convictions but Hall liked his job too much for Wright to ruin it all. Hall devised a plan to take Wright on a rabbit hunt under the pretence of coming to an agreement.

While in the woods, Hall shot Wright dead and buried him in a shallow grave next to a stream in the grounds of the estate. But Wright had already told Margaret Hudson of Hall's criminal past, and Hall was fired.

Immediately moving down to Chelsea, London, Hall found work as a butler at the penthouse apartment of retired labour politician Walter Scott-Elliott and his Indian-born wife, Dorothy, who had wealth beyond compare.

Three months into the job, he came up with a plan to rob the Scott-Elliott's of their fortune and elope to a foreign non-extradition country. On 8th December 1977, Hall and an accomplice named Michael Kitto went to the apartment to view the antiques, in order to price things up.

Hall believed that Walter would be in bed and Dorothy was getting treatment at a nearby nursing home but as they discussed their plans of how to cash in the goods and rob the apartment of everything, Dorothy walked in on them – and heard what they were planning.

Kitto and Hall pounced on Dorothy, and Kitto suffocated her to death with a pillow but it has long remained unclear whether Hall was the culprit in her murder. The pair carried her body to the bedroom and put her in bed as if she had died in her sleep.

They then drugged Walter, who was curious to know what had happened to his wife, and he passed out on his bed. The next morning, Kitto and Hall recruited a 51-year-old sex worker named Mary Coggle and came up with an audacious plan.

Bloody road trip

Hall believed they could pass off Coggle as the late Dorothy, hoping that Walter, who would be drugged up, would believe Coggle to be his wife. They put Dorothy's body in the boot of the car the next day and sat Walter next to Coggle in the back seat, then drove north towards Scotland with all of the couple's antiques and riches.

They stopped at various financial establishments where Walter, under guidance from Coggle, emptied the Scott-Elliot bank accounts. They drugged Walter so heavily that he had to be helped to their pit-stop accommodation in Cumbria before travelling to Perthshire the next day. The pair buried Dorothy in a shallow grave and continued northward.

After having Walter sign some documents giving them further access to the Scott-Elliot financial accounts, they drove to Glen Affric in the Highlands, where Hall and Kitto murdered Walter by strangling and beating him to death. They buried his body in remote woodland near Inverness.

The trio decided to return to London after selling off some of the antiques across Scotland but Coggle was becoming too accustomed to her newfound life of luxury. She took to wearing Dorothy's fur coat everywhere which Hall thought was going to attract attention.

When Coggle refused to get rid of the coat, Hall killed her with a poker stick and left her body in a stream in Dumfriesshire, which was found a few days later on Christmas Day 1977. Hall and Kitto travelled to Hall's holiday home in Cumbria, only to find that Hall's brother, convicted paedophile, Donald, had been released from jail and was sitting in the living room.

Hotel mishap

Hall hated Donald for what he had done to be convicted, so he tied him to a chair, used chloroform to knock him out, then drowned him in the bath with Kitto's help. The murder was later recognised as the first murder resulting from chloroform in the United Kingdom.

The pair put Donald's body in the boot of the car and again drove northward to Scotland, where they checked into the Blenheim House Hotel in North Berwick, near Edinburgh. As the pair were drinking in the hotel bar, the manager became suspicious of them as they were acting unusually jumpy.

Believing they would elope the following morning without paying, the manager called the police who checked the numberplate of Hall's car. To hide the identity of the owner, Hall had changed the number plate as it contained three nine's which he believed was unlucky.

The police check showed the numberplate, car, and tax disc didn't match, and arrested Kitto, who was taken in for questioning. Hall had managed to escape through a toilet window but was caught shortly after at a police roadblock. Not realising what was in the boot of the car, police moved the vehicle to the storage area of the local police station, where they discovered Donald's body.

At the same time, in London, police were investigating the disappearances of the Scott-Elliot's and a suspected robbery that had taken place in their apartment. Police in Scotland traced the car to London and linked up with London police, connecting both crimes.

The not-so perfect gentleman

Soon enough, Hall confessed to everything and led police to the graves of his victims. The murder of Coggle was connected to Hall after he confessed to killing her. After a failed suicide attempt, Hall realised he was in for a lengthy sentence.

He also confessed that he had planned to kill Kitto, which is why he was acting fidgety at the hotel that night. Throughout 1978, both men appeared at different trials in Scotland and England, as the murders had taken place in two separate countries.

Hall was ultimately convicted of four murders and confirmed to have murdered Dorothy but her case didn't go to trial as the judge said it would not have affected the ultimate outcome of life imprisonment. Kitto was sentenced to life for three murders.

As time progressed and parole dates beckoned, various home secretaries ordered that Hall remain in prison under a whole life tariff. Hall died of natural causes in Kingston Prison, Portsmouth, in 2002, aged 78.

Michael Kitto was released after his minimum term of 15 years in prison, in 1992. What happened to him afterwards is not public knowledge, but it is suspected he was set up with a new identity to live out the rest of his days in freedom.

FACTS!

In 1941, Hall volunteered for the Red Cross charity organisation where he had a fling with a Polish freedom fighter.

Hall published an autobiography in 1999 called 'The Perfect Gentleman', which can still be bought today.

Archibald Hall was the oldest prisoner to be serving a whole life tariff when he died.

The Ice Cream Wars

In 1980s Glasgow, rival criminal gangs were using ice cream vans to sell drugs and stolen goods, leading to the mass murder of six people and a man gluing himself to the railings of Buckingham Palace.

The Ice Cream Wars in Glasgow during the early 1980s resulted in mass murder, a 20-year long court case and bizarre behaviour from some of the people involved. It was one of the strangest yet most violent periods of Glasgow's history and was no place or time to be peddling ice cream.

From the 1960s in Glasgow, large housing projects were built, including the infamous Red Road site. Many of the sprawling council blocks had no additional development on them, which meant no supermarkets or other shops. This forced people to travel out of the developments to get what they needed.

To fulfil the need of the residents, ice cream van owners began repurposing their vehicles to sell groceries, including all the basics, along with newspapers and toilet paper. Very few at the time were actually selling ice creams.

The idea was that instead of having residents travel to a supermarket, the ice cream vans could come to them, negating the need for leaving the blocks. Some of the van owners were making a reasonable living but quickly discovered that if they sold contraband like cigarettes from abroad or stolen alcohol then they could make even more money.

Some of the vans decided that alongside selling Cornetto's and Magnums, they could bring in even more money by selling illegal drugs. This caught the attention of some of Glasgow's gangs in the early 1980s, who were looking for an easy way into some of the developments, as they were profitable locations to be in control of.

Serious Chimes Squad

As the gangs began infiltrating the ice cream vans, the once happy jingles coming out of the van's speakers meant that drugs were on the way into the estates. Soon, a battle began for control of the estates and that meant whoever owned or utilised the most ice cream vans was going to be bringing in the most profits.

Soon enough, Glasgow's Serious Crimes Squad, who were referred to as the Serious Chimes Squad, began to cotton on that the vans were being used to smuggle drugs in and out of the estates. And soon enough, the Ice Cream Wars were in full effect.

Stories began emerging of ice cream van drivers attacking other vans with bricks and planks of wood, hoping to end the other's business. Many drivers, some of whom were not involved, began storing knives and axes in their vans out of fear of being attacked or accosted by the gangs.

With the knowledge that some ice cream vans carried drugs and other contraband, petty criminals began attacking vans to loot them. If they just so happened to attack a van that was run by one of the larger gangs, then the gangs retaliated with violence.

In the early 1980s, industry in Glasgow was collapsing at an unprecedented rate, leaving mass unemployment in the city. This led to public unrest and massive poverty, not helped by the sprawling estates gifted to them from the 1960s. Then, in 1984, the Ice Cream Wars came to a head when six people were murdered in an arson attack.

Mass murder

An 18-year-old ice cream van driver named Andrew Doyle was merely trying to keep his family above the poverty line by selling ice creams and other home goods. Despite being shot at while in his van one day, he had refused all the gang's advances to peddle drugs through his business.

He was warned by one of the gangs that he didn't have permission to operate on the housing estates but he ignored the warnings, which made him enemies. He was intimidated, threatened, shot at, and assaulted but still refused to stand down.

At around 2am on 16th April 1984, the gangs decided to frighten Doyle into working for them and targeted his Ruchazie property for an arson attack. The door of the property was doused in petrol and set alight. There were nine people staying in the property that night, and the resulting blaze killed six members of the Doyle family, including Andrew.

The six victims were James Doyle, 53, his daughter Christina Halleron, 25, her 18-month-old son Mark, and three of James' sons, James Jr., 23, Tony, 14, and Andrew. The mass murder shocked Scotland and the public quickly learned of the ice cream wars that were taking place in the country's largest city.

The police, who were already seen as inept in the eyes of the public, came under scrutiny as having failed to control gang violence in the city. Under pressure to bring justice to the Doyle family and Scotland, the police arrested many people in the months that followed including two men who spent 20 years proclaiming their innocence.

A witness, a statement, and a map of Glasgow

Four people were tried and convicted of offences relating to the ice cream wars. Two more, Thomas Campbell and Joe Steele were charged with the arson attack, convicted of murder, and sentenced to life in prison, with the judge handing down an order of a 20-year minimum term. Campbell was also convicted of the shooting of Doyle's van and given an additional 10 years.

What followed was a 20-year long court battle that involved hunger strikes, prison breakouts, political pandering, solitary isolation, prison beatings, appeals, and a belief that the police had ended up arresting two innocent men.

The case against Campbell and Steele rested on three main pieces of evidence, a witness, a statement, and a map of Glasgow with an X where Doyle's house was. The witness, William Love, claimed that he had overheard Campbell and Steele talking about arson while drinking in a city centre bar, and stated that they wanted to teach Doyle a lesson.

The police stated that Campbell had made a statement in which he said, '*I only wanted the van shot up. The fire at Fat Boy's was only meant to be a frightener which went too far.*' The photocopied map of Glasgow with an X where Doyle's house sat, was found in Campbell's flat following his arrest.

Campbell was known to have been involved in the ice cream wars since 1983 and was keen to protect his patch against rival gang members. He was known as an enforcer, and Steele was his sidekick, recruited by Campbell for his campaign against rival gangs.

Both men claimed they had been set up by the witness, William Love, as he worked for a rival gang in secret, and that the evidence against them was falsified by police, including the map found in Campbell's flat.

Glued to Buckingham Palace

Campbell denied he had given a statement to police and that it had been constructed by them with the sole purpose of convicting someone for the Doyle murders. An appeal in 1989, five years after their conviction, failed to overturn their sentences.

In 1992, two journalists, Douglas Skelton and Lisa Brownlie, wrote a book about the ice cream wars entitled *Frightener*. In it, they interviewed William Love, who told them he had lied under oath for the simple reason that it suited his own selfish purposes and that the police pressured him to give evidence against Campbell.

What followed were a succession of failed appeals and Steele going to great lengths to prove his innocence. He went on a hunger strike several times and let his hair grow long. While he was allowed to visit his mother, he eloped from the prison officers, who later found him on a roof with banners claiming he was innocent.

Steele escaped from prison twice more, with the third and final time coming when he and four other inmates slipped through a wire fence during an outdoor exercise period. Steele travelled all the way to London to make a high-profile demonstration.

He made his way to Buckingham Palace where he superglued himself to the railings outside of the building. His plight made national news, and in some respects, the unusual demonstration brought massive public attention to his plight.

While he was glued to the railings, he told a journalist, *'if I had murdered the Doyle's, I would have admitted it and done my time quietly and without any fuss, to get an early release. I cannot admit guilt or show remorse for something I didn't do.'*

City of culture

The Buckingham Palace incident caused the British Secretary of State to refer the case to the appeal court. But the three judges reached a split decision which sent Campbell and Steele back to prison. After many more appeals, the pair's lawyers referred the case to the Scottish Criminal Cases Review Commission.

Three years later, in 2004, a new appeal court overturned the convictions, mostly on the basis of the flawed witness account from William Love and what the appeal court called significant misdirection of the jury. It was also concluded that Campbell's fake statement had been created by police in error, though many now see it as being constructed purely for the purpose of securing a conviction. In essence, the court of appeal decided the jury in the original trial was wrong.

Campbell and Steele walked out of court as free men in 2004, 20 years after the Doyle arson attack. Campbell and Steele later accused Glasgow gang boss Tam McGraw, who died in 2007, of being behind the arson attack, and that Tam had instigated a 20-year long campaign to keep them behind bars.

No new investigation into the Doyle murders was opened and the crime remains a stain on Glasgow's history. Some residents will never forget the time that ice cream vans were peddling drugs within the city limits.

FACTS!

Glasgow held the Commonwealth Games in 2014 with 71 nations taking part and 5,000 athletes.

Glasgow was designated the European City of Culture in 1990 and remains the only Scottish city to have done so.

The city of Glasgow includes 12% of Scotland's entire population but accounts for 18% of all recorded crime in the country.

That's Not Cocaine!

Believing they had stumbled upon a goldmine, three thieves stole two large jars of cocaine, but after snorting it, they realised they were urns that contained the ashes of one human and two dogs.

Some thieves are considered masterminds, planning the ultimate robbery of expensive art pieces, the perfect bank robbery, or a job that no one else could pull off. But on 15th December 2011, three thieves went in the opposite direction and fell into the realm of the dumbest thieves to have ever lived.

It sounds like a scene from one of the Dumb and Dumber movies, where bumbling idiots break into a house and steal two jars full of cocaine, not realising they were actually the ashes of one human and two dogs. But that's exactly what happened in Silver Springs Shores in Florida.

And not only did they steal the jars believing they held cocaine, but they actually snorted a vast majority of it before realising something was drastically wrong. It was only then they decided to get rid of the jars, not knowing at the time what exactly they had snorted – or who!

Friends and petty criminals, 19-year-olds Waldo Soroa and Jose David Diaz Marrero, and 18-year-old Matrix Andaluz, decided to up their criminal status and move to robbing houses in the middle of the night.

This led them to the home of an English housewife, 35-year-old Holli Tencza. For the three thieves, it would be their first big job in the hope it would bring great riches and allow them to move up the criminal ladder, but it backfired in a big way.

Lines of ashes

Though we're unsure why three young thieves believed the urns to be full of cocaine or heroin, they stole them, nonetheless. They approached the house in the middle of the night and entered through a back door where they were met with no resistance.

They focused on the usual hauls; electrical items, jewellery and priceless possessions, before one of the three found the jars on a shelf and had a quick peek inside. Believing them to be full of enticing white powder, the thief thought he had hit the jackpot and added them to the haul.

Before eloping, one of the thieves noticed photographs of two Great Danes but there were no dogs in sight. It didn't click then that they had made off with the dogs ashes but it was about to. They fled the home with their haul and went back to Waldo's residence.

They counted their haul and worked out rough prices for what they could sell them at before turning their attention to the jars of priceless white powder. So full of belief they were that the jars contained cocaine that they spooned out some of the contents and made lines on the table in front of them.

One by one, they reached over and snorted a line. Only then did it hit them that something was wrong but it didn't stop them trying again. They cut three more lines and snorted them again but they weren't getting the hit they were used to.

Enter their friend and fellow petty criminal, Gabriel Ruiz, who walked in on the trio snorting the lines. After a quick look at what they had stolen, he sat next to them with a look of confusion on his face and asked them why they were snorting ashes from an urn.

Crazy world

The three thieves initially didn't want to believe it but with the way the lines weren't hitting right and the fact the jars looked like urn jars, it suddenly dawned on them they had been snorting the ashes of cremated bodies.

Memories of the photos of the dogs came rushing back and they realised they had just ingested dead dogs. But not only that, though one of the jars did indeed contain the ashes of two Great Danes, the other contained the ashes of Holli's late father.

When Holli woke up the next morning to find her home had been ransacked, she was distraught and called police. Later that day, she spoke to a local newspaper and said the following.

'I understand why the burglar took my flat-screen television, the Blu-ray DVD player, laptop computer and jewellery, but there's no monetary value in the ashes, so who knows in this crazy world. I just want them back. I don't care if I ever know who took them.'

When the thieves learned what it was they had stolen, they were met with pangs of guilt and wanted to anonymously return the urns to Holli. But Ruiz and another friend who was too young to be named said it would be foolish as their fingerprints would be all over them.

Ruiz convinced them to throw the urns into the local Magic Lake in Gail d'Helvie Park, which they did. A week later, police closed in on them after witness statements put them near Holli's home the night of the robbery, and they were arrested the following day.

Following the thieves confessions, divers searched the lake and discovered the two urns that still had partial fingerprint matches for the trio. Remarkably, the ashes were protected by plastic bags inside treated wooden boxes stored in the urns and they were intact.

The ashes were returned to Holli relatively unscathed, save for the missing lines the trio had snorted. For Waldo, Jose David, and Matrix, they were hit with the long arm of the law and jailed for the burglary along with other criminal charges. They will go down forever as possibly the dumbest thieves in Florida.

FACTS!

European scientists first isolated cocaine from coca leaves in the 1850s and claimed it was a medical wonder drug, but it's now known as one of the most addictive substances on Earth.

Coca-Cola was founded in 1886 and was originally created from a concoction of cocaine and sugary syrup. Cocaine was removed as an ingredient in 1903.

Sigmund Freud was a fan and advocate of cocaine and wrote an essay in which he praised it as a magical substance – before becoming addicted to it for 12 long years.

Bonus material

Bitesize Extras

Lightsaber Attack

A week before Christmas in 2011, in Portland, Oregon, police were called to the city's branch of Toys R Us. The reason: a man was wandering around the shop attacking customers with a Star Wars lightsaber toy.

33-year-old David Canterbury, who lived in nearby Hillsboro, had simply had enough of Christmas and decided to swing his lightsaber at every customer he could find. When he wasn't able to be talked down by police, he was tased.

But David, being an extraordinary Jedi, literally broke the taser wires using the lightsaber, forcing police to jump on him and bring him under control. He was taken to a nearby psychiatric hospital where he underwent mental health evaluation.

Oregon forums were full of posts about the story, with some eagle-eyed Star Wars fans noticing that David was wielding a blue lightsaber – the colour of the Jedi, which meant he hadn't fully turned to the dark side, at least, not yet.

DUI in a Barbie Car

40-year-old former RAF engineer, Paul Hutton, was arrested in the Spring of 2010 in Essex, England, after being caught driving a Barbie car under the influence. He had found the Barbie car ten years earlier abandoned on the side of the road and had spent the previous year rebuilding it.

He installed larger wheels and a larger battery putting its top speed at a massive 4mph. On March 28th, a drunken Paul climbed into the Barbie car, which involved great feats of contortionism and decided to drive to a friend's house a few blocks away to show it off.

Unfortunately for him, a passing police car saw him on the road with his knees tucked under his chin and asked him to pullover. Despite only going 4mph, Paul attempted to outrun police – as the officers left the car and walked alongside him.

He was ultimately arrested for not pulling over and then for drink-driving when they performed a breathalyser test on him. Paul was convicted of driving under the influence, banned from driving, and given a 12-month conditional discharge. Moral of the story: don't drive kid's cars drunk.

Fully-Clothed Robber Hides in Nudist Resort

In Kissimmee, Florida, in May 2012, Milton Hodges decided to try and rob Lowe's home improvement store. He told staff he was looking to buy mango and banana trees before holding a staff member hostage with a pair of scissors to their neck.

Eagle-eyed customers saw what was happening and chased Hodges out of the store. An hour later, he was seen climbing the wall of the Cypress Cove Nudist Resort, in an attempt to hide, not realising it was a nudist resort.

He stole a golf buggy at knife point from the security guard and drove to the nudist area of the resort. Except, he forgot to remove his clothes.

When police arrived to search the resort, they found the fully-clothed Hodges attempting to hide among a group of nude holidaymakers. Hodges was convicted of 10 crimes relating to his afternoon and evening of crime and stupidity.

Bibliography

A selected bibliography and resource.

Anderson, Delonda (2019) *The Devil in Appalachia: The Bloodthirsty Harpe Brothers.* https://www.appalachiabare.com/the-devil-in-appalachia-the-bloodthirsty-harpe-brothers Appalachia Bare.

AP News (1989) *Officials Puzzled Over Woman's Appearance But Rule Out Kidnapping.* https://apnews.com/article/2dbf23e69af1b06aa283399f15dcc45d. AP News.

Bell, Amy (2014) *Murder Capital: Suspicious deaths in London*. Manchester University Press, ISBN: 9780719091971

Blackburn, May Otis (1936) *The Origin of God.* DeVross & Company.

Carr, Todd (2019) *Cave-in-Rock Pirates and Outlaws*. History Press Library Editions. ISBN: 9781540238818.

Desborough, Jenny (2020) *Kirsty MacColl death: How did Kirsty MacColl die? Cause of death.* The Daily Express.

Eatwell, Piu (2018) *Black Dahlia, Red Rose*. Coronet. ISBN: 9781473666344.

Edition, Inside (2019) *Family Mourns Mother Stabbed, Bludgeoned to Death in Church Nearly 3 Years Ago.* https://www.insideedition.com/family-mourns-mother-stabbed-bludgeoned-death-church-nearly-3-years-ago-50829 Inside Edition.

Engelhaupt, Erika. (2021) *How science solved the mystery of feet washing ashore in the Pacific Northwest.* https://www.nationalgeographic.com/science/article/how-science-solved-the-mystery-of-feet-washing-ashore-in-the-pacific-northwest-salish-sea. National Geographic.

FBI (2022) *Murder and Mayhem in the Osage Hills.* https://www.fbi.gov/history/famous-cases/murder-and-mayhem-in-the-osage-hills FBI

Fitts, Alexis Sobel (2016) *I know who killed the Black Dahlia: my own father.* https://www.theguardian.com/us-news/2016/may/26/black-dahlia-murder-steve-hodel-elizabeth-short The Guardian.

Fort, Samuel (2014) *Cult of the Great Eleven.* CreateSpace. ISBN: 9781502782588.

Gilmore, John (2006/1994) *Severed: The True Story of the Black Dahlia Murder.* Los Angeles: Amok Books. ISBN: 9781878923103.

Hall, Roy Archibald. Holt, Trevor Anthony. (2002) *To Kill and Kill Again: The Chilling True Confessions of a Serial Killer.* John Blake Publishing. ISBN: 9781857825558

Hodel, Steve (2003) *Black Dahlia Avenger: A Genius for Murder.* New York: Arcade Publishing. ISBN: 1559706643.

Jeffrey, Robert (2002) *Gangland Glasgow: True Crime from the Streets.* Black and White Publishing. ISBN 1902927591

Keen, Liz (2016) *Thieves who targeted Jammie Dodger factory stealing £20,000-worth of treats are jailed.* Walesonline.co.uk Media Wales Ltd.

NZ Herald (2003) *Man hacked brother to death over dinner slight.* https://www.nzherald.co.nz/nz/man-hacked-brother-to-death-over-dinner-slight/PHCZ25I2ZYDP5RH3GKMCDASMRI/ New Zealand Herald.

Osage Nation, The. (2022) https://www.osagenation-nsn.gov/ *The Osage Nation website.*

Read, Simon (2006) *In the Dark: The True Story of the Blackout Ripper.* Berkley Publishing Group. ISBN: 9780425212837

Reuters (2011) *Burglars snort man's ashes thought it was cocaine.* https://www.reuters.com/article/us-ashes-odd-idUSTRE70I6KR20110119 Reuters.

Rosen, Fred (2005) *The Historical Atlas of American Crime.* New York: Facts on File. ISBN: 9781438129853.

Solomons, Adams (2021) *Evil 'vampire' killer sucked corpses' blood in morgues then turned to alive victims.* https://www.dailystar.co.uk/news/world-news/evil-vampire-killer-sucked-corpses-24430307 The Daily Star.

Steele, Tom (2016) *Slain fitness instructor Missy Bevers received 'creepy and strange' message days before death, search warrant says.* The Dallas Morning News.

Stuff NZ. (2017) *Fergus Glen denied parole for murdering brother in Wainuiomata.*
https://www.stuff.co.nz/national/crime/92721588/fergus-glen-denied-parole-for-murdering-brother-in-wainuiomata. Stuff.co.nz

Sulway, Verity (2021) *Fairytale of New York singer Kirsty MacColl's horror speedboat death after saving son.* The Daily Mirror.

Visit Lancaster (2022) *Pendle Witch Trail.*
https://visitlancaster.org.uk/things-to-do/pendle-witch-trail-lancaster-to-pendle/ Visit Lancaster.

Photo and image credits:

Look for more in the Bizarre True Crime Series from Ben Oakley & Twelvetrees Camden

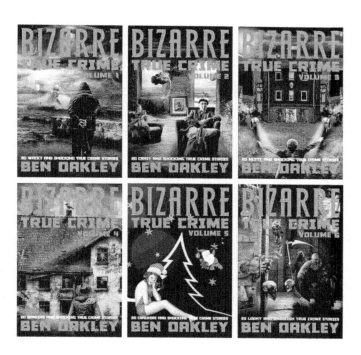

OUT NOW!

Fancy TWO true crime books for FREE?

Visit www.benoakley.co.uk and download today!

Printed in Great Britain
by Amazon